200 Lig
gluten-free recipes

hamlyn | **all colour cookbook**

200 Light
gluten-free recipes

An Hachette UK Company
www.hachette.co.uk

First published in Great Britain in 2015 by
Hamlyn, a division of Octopus Publishing Group Ltd
Carmelite House
50 Victoria Embankment
London EC4Y 0DZ
www.octopusbooks.co.uk

Recipes in this book have previously appeared in other books
published by Hamlyn.

ISBN 978-0-600-63213-9

A CIP catalogue record for this book is available from the
British Library.

Printed and bound in China

1 2 3 4 5 6 7 8 9 10

Standard level spoon measurements are used in all recipes.
1 tablespoon = one 15 ml spoon
1 teaspoon = one 5 ml spoon

Both imperial and metric measurements have been given in
all recipes. Use one set of measurements only and not a
mixture of both.

Ovens should be preheated to the specific temperature – if using a
fan-assisted oven, follow manufacturer's instructions for adjusting
the time and the temperature.

Eggs should be medium unless otherwise stated. The Department
of Health advises that eggs should not be consumed raw. This book
contains dishes made with raw or lightly cooked eggs. It is prudent
for more vulnerable people such as pregnant and nursing mothers,
invalids, the elderly, babies and young children to avoid uncooked or
lightly cooked dishes made with eggs. Once prepared these dishes
should be kept refrigerated and used promptly.

Milk should be full fat unless otherwise stated.

Fresh herbs should be used unless otherwise stated. If unavailable
use dried herbs as an alternative but halve the quantities stated.

Pepper should be freshly ground black pepper unless
otherwise stated.

This book includes dishes made with nuts and nut derivatives.
It is advisable for customers with known allergic reactions to nuts
and nut derivatives and those who may be potentially vulnerable
to these allergies, such as pregnant and nursing mothers, invalids,
the elderly, babies and children, to avoid dishes made with nuts
and nut oils. It is also prudent to check the labels of pre-prepared
ingredients for the possible inclusion of nut derivatives.

Vegetarians should look for the 'V' symbol on a cheese to ensure
it is made with vegetarian rennet.

contents

introduction

introduction

this series

The Hamlyn All Colour Light Series is a collection of handy-sized books, each packed with over 200 healthy recipes on a variety of topics and cuisines to suit your needs.

The books are designed to help those people who are trying to lose weight by offering a range of delicious recipes that are low in calories but still high in flavour. The recipes show the calorie count per portion, so you will know exactly what you are eating. These are recipes for real and delicious food, not ultra-slimming meals, so they will help you maintain your new, healthier eating plan for life. They must be used as part of a balanced diet, with the cakes and sweet dishes eaten only as an occasional treat.

how to use this book

All the recipes in this book are clearly marked with the number of calories (kcal) per serving. The chapters cover different calorie bands: under 500 calories, under 400 calories, etc.

There are variations of each recipe at the bottom of the page – note the calorie count as they do vary and can sometimes be more than the original recipe.

The figures assume that you are using low-fat versions of dairy products, so be sure to use skimmed milk and low-fat yogurt. They have also been calculated using lean meat, so make sure you trim meat of all visible fat and remove the skin from chicken breasts.

Use moderate amounts of oil and butter for cooking and low-fat/low-calorie alternatives when you can.

Don't forget to take note of the number of portions each recipe makes and divide up the quantity of food accordingly, so that you know exactly how many calories you are consuming. Be careful about side dishes and accompaniments as they will add to the calorie content.

Above all, enjoy trying out the new flavours and exciting recipes that this book contains. Rather than dwelling on the thought that you are denying yourself your usual unhealthy treats, think of your new regime as a positive step towards a new you. Not only will you lose weight and feel more confident, but your

health will benefit, the condition of your hair and nails will improve, and you will take on a healthy glow.

the risks of obesity

Up to half of women and two-thirds of men are overweight or obese in the developed world today. Being overweight not only can make us unhappy with our appearance, but can also lead to serious health problems, including heart disease, high blood pressure and diabetes.

When someone is obese, it means they are overweight to the point that it could start to seriously threaten their health. In fact, obesity ranks as a close second to smoking as a possible cause of cancer. Obese women are more likely to have complications during and after pregnancy, and people who are overweight or obese are also more likely to suffer from coronary heart disease, gallstones, osteoarthritis, high blood pressure and type 2 diabetes.

how can I tell if I am overweight?

The best way to tell if you are overweight is to work out your body mass index (BMI). If using metric measurements, divide your weight in kilograms (kg) by your height in metres (m) squared. (For example, if you are 1.7 m tall and weigh 70 kg, the calculation would be $70 \div 2.89 = 24.2$.) If using imperial measurements, divide your weight in pounds

(lb) by your height in inches (in) squared and multiply by 703. Then compare the figure to the list below (these figures apply to healthy adults only).

Less than 20	underweight
20–25	healthy
25–30	overweight
Over 30	obese

As we all know by now, one of the major causes of obesity is eating too many calories.

what is a calorie?

Our bodies need energy to stay alive, grow, keep warm and be active. We get the energy we need to survive from the food and drinks we consume – more specifically, from the fat, carbohydrate, protein and alcohol that they contain.

A calorie (cal), as anyone who has ever been on a diet will know, is the unit used to measure how much energy different foods contain. A calorie can be scientifically defined as the energy required to raise the temperature of 1 gram of water from 14.5°C

to 15.5°C. A kilocalorie (kcal) is 1,000 calories and it is, in fact, kilocalories that we usually mean when we talk about the calories in different foods.

Different food types contain different numbers of calories. For example, a gram of carbohydrate (starch or sugar) provides 3.75 kcal, protein provides 4 kcal per gram, fat provides 9 kcal per gram and alcohol provides 7 kcal per gram. So, fat is the most concentrated source of energy – weight for weight, it provides just over twice as many calories as either protein or carbohydrate – with alcohol not far behind. The energy content of a food or drink depends on how many grams of carbohydrate, fat, protein and alcohol are present.

how many calories do we need?

The number of calories we need to consume varies from person to person, but your body weight is a clear indication of whether you are eating the right amount. Body weight is simply determined by the number of calories you are eating compared to the number of calories your body is using to maintain itself and needed for physical activity. If you regularly consume more calories than you use up, you will start to gain weight as extra energy is stored in the body as fat.

Based on our relatively inactive modern-day lifestyles, most nutritionists recommend that women should aim to consume around 2,000 calories (kcal) per day, and men an amount of around 2,500. Of course, the amount of energy required depends on your level of activity: the more active you are, the more energy you need to maintain a stable weight.

a healthier lifestyle

To maintain a healthy body weight, we need to expend as much energy as we eat; to lose weight, energy expenditure must therefore exceed intake of calories. So, exercise is a vital tool in the fight to lose weight. Physical activity doesn't just help us control body weight; it also helps to reduce our appetite and is known to have beneficial effects on the heart and blood that help protect against cardiovascular disease.

Many of us claim we don't enjoy exercise and simply don't have the time to fit it into our hectic schedules, so the easiest way to increase physical activity is by incorporating it into our daily routines, perhaps by walking or cycling instead of driving (particularly for short journeys), taking up more active hobbies such as gardening, and taking small and simple steps, such as using the stairs instead of the lift whenever possible.

As a general guide, adults should aim to undertake at least 30 minutes of moderate-intensity exercise, such as a brisk walk, five times a week. The 30 minutes does not have to be taken all at once: three sessions of 10 minutes are equally beneficial. Children and young people should be encouraged to take at least 60 minutes of moderate-intensity exercise every day.

Some activities will use up more energy than others. The following list shows some examples of the energy a person weighing 60 kg (132 lb) would expend doing the following activities for 30 minutes:

activity	energy
Ironing	69 kcal
Cleaning	75 kcal
Walking	99 kcal
Golf	129 kcal
Fast walking	150 kcal
Cycling	180 kcal
Aerobics	195 kcal
Swimming	195 kcal
Running	300 kcal
Sprinting	405 kcal

2,000 per day thereafter to maintain her new body weight. Regular exercise will also make a huge difference: the more you can burn, the less you will need to diet.

improve your diet

For most of us, simply adopting a more balanced diet will reduce our calorie intake and lead to weight loss. Follow these simple recommendations:

Eat more starchy foods, such as bread, potatoes, rice and pasta. Assuming these replace the fattier foods you usually eat, and you don't smother them with oil or butter, this will help reduce the amount of fat and increase the amount of fibre in your diet. As a bonus, try to use wholegrain rice, pasta and flour, as the energy from these foods is released more slowly in the body, making you feel fuller for longer.

Eat more fruit and vegetables, aiming for at least five portions of different fruit and vegetables a day (excluding potatoes).

As long as you don't add extra fat to your fruit and vegetables in the form of cream, butter or oil, these changes will help reduce your fat intake and increase the amount of fibre and vitamins you consume.

who said vegetables must be dull?

Eat fewer sugary foods, such as biscuits, cakes and chocolate bars. This will also help reduce your fat intake. If you fancy something sweet, aim for fresh or dried fruit instead.

make changes for life

The best way to lose weight is to try to adopt healthier eating habits that you can easily maintain all the time, not just when you are trying to slim down. Aim to lose no more than 1 kg (2 lb) per week to ensure you lose only your fat stores. People who go on crash diets lose lean muscle as well as fat and are much more likely to put the weight back on again soon afterwards.

For a woman, the aim is to reduce her daily calorie intake to around 1,500 kcal while she is trying to lose weight, then settle on around

Reduce the amount of fat in your diet, so you consume fewer calories. Choosing low-fat versions of dairy products, such as skimmed milk and low-fat yogurt, doesn't necessarily mean your food will be tasteless. Low-fat versions are available for most dairy products, including milk, cheese, crème fraîche, yogurt, and even cream and butter.

Choose lean cuts of meat, such as back bacon instead of streaky, and chicken breasts instead of thighs. Trim all visible fat off meat before cooking and avoid frying foods – grill or roast instead. Fish is also naturally low in fat and can make a variety of tempting dishes.

simple steps to reduce your intake

Few of us have an iron will, so when you are trying to cut down make it easier on yourself by following these steps:

- Serve small portions to start with. You may feel satisfied when you have finished, but if you are still hungry you can always go back for more.
- Once you have served up your meal, put away any leftover food before you eat. Don't put heaped serving dishes on the table as you will undoubtedly pick, even if you feel satisfied with what you have already eaten.
- Eat slowly and savour your food; then you are more likely to feel full when you have finished. If you rush a meal, you may still feel hungry afterwards.
- Make an effort with your meals. Just because you are cutting down doesn't mean your

meals have to be low on taste as well as calories. You will feel more satisfied with a meal you have really enjoyed and will be less likely to look for comfort in a bag of crisps or a bar of chocolate.

- Plan your meals in advance to make sure you have all the ingredients you need. Searching the cupboards when you are hungry is unlikely to result in a healthy, balanced meal.
- Keep healthy and interesting snacks to hand for those moments when you need something to pep you up. You don't need to succumb to a chocolate bar if there are other tempting treats on offer.

what is gluten and why should you avoid it?

This book aims to show you not only how you can cook foods to avoid eating gluten, but also how to eat low-calorie foods to enable you to loose or maintain your weight in a controlled and healthy way. There are plenty of gluten-free foods available to buy in supermarkets, but these are not always healthy or low in calories, so cooking ingredients from scratch is sometimes preferable, and this book shows that it can be tasty, easy and usually cheaper, too.

Gluten is the general name for proteins found in wheat, rye and barley, and although it has been part of the human diet for thousands of years, an increasing number of people suffer a negative reaction to it, especially those suffering from coeliac disease.

Coeliac disease is an autoimmune disease that affects 1 in 100 people in the UK – symptoms include chronic diarrhoea, weight loss, abdominal pain, joint pain and fatigue. Gluten triggers an immune response that causes damage to the intestines, leaving people unable to absorb nutrients from food, which in turn can lead to more serious, life-threatening problems. There is no known cure and the best treatment is to follow a gluten-free diet for life.

Millions of people who don't have coeliac disease still suffer negative symptoms after eating gluten – this is referred to as 'gluten intolerance' and it occurs when a person's immune system responds abnormally when gluten is digested, causing uncomfortable symptoms such as bloating, abdominal pain and heartburn.

If you are not sure if your symptoms relate to gluten, it is best to avoid all foods that contain gluten (see below), then gradually reintroduce them to your diet to assess your body's reaction.

foods to avoid

Gluten is found in wheat, rye, barley and any foods made with these grains, such as:
• White flour

- Whole-wheat flour
- Durum wheat
- Kamut
- Spelt
- Semolina
- Wheat bran
- Wheat germ

Processed foods that contain gluten also include:
- Couscous
- Pasta
- Bread
- Flour tortillas
- Cakes
- Muffins
- Biscuits
- Crackers
- Cereals
- Beer
- Gravy
- Dressings
- Sauces
- Pastries
- Baking powder
- Foods in batter

Foods that may also contain gluten but are less obvious include:
- Soy sauce
- Matzo
- Ready-made soups
- Stock cubes
- Some confectionery
- Hot dogs

- Seasoned chips or snacks
- Ready-made salad dressings
- Sausages

This list of foods to avoid is by no means a definitive list as products change every day, so it's very important if you are buying processed foods to read the labels thoroughly (another good reason to cook your own foods from scratch!). It's also important to remember that wheat-free does not mean gluten-free, as the food may still contain traces of rye or barley.

Cross-contamination can also occur with some foods, so again it's important to check labels carefully. For example, pure oats are gluten-free but most commercially processed oats may be contaminated during growing, harvesting or processing so, again, check labels thoroughly.

15

so what can you eat?

It may seem like there is a lot you cannot have, but it's better to focus on all the great ingredients you can eat! There are now lots of gluten-free bread, pasta, biscuit and cake products available to buy, but you can also make your own, or substitute with something else. For example, instead of pasta try quinoa or rice, stock up on great fresh fruit and vegetables, and use spices and herbs to add great flavours.

If you love baking and can't bear the thought of living without cake or biscuits (and luckily you don't need to!), there are also lots of gluten-free flours available – for example, rice, gram, almond, buckwheat, chestnut, tapioca and coconut – as well as gluten-free baking powder and bicarbonate of soda. The recipes in this book have been tested using gluten-free flours, but be aware that these flours act differently to normal flour, so you may need to experiment if

adapting other recipes. It's probably best to avoid recipes that rely on flour as the main ingredient, or use ground almonds with gluten-free flours to help give a bit of 'moisture' (*see* Cottage Cheese & Chive Muffins on page 126), as gluten-free flours are very dry.

To begin with, eating gluten-free may seem really difficult, but once you get to grips with new ingredients you will find it can be just as simple and satisfying as eating a gluten-rich diet. Remember to seek out naturally gluten-free foods (meat, fish, seafood, eggs, dairy, legumes and pulses), as there are lots of them. Although grains that carry gluten are out, there are many naturally gluten-free grains – such as quinoa, millet, amaranth, flax and chia – that you can enjoy in a variety of ways. For recipes using quinoa, for example, try the Quinoa & Lamb Stuffed Peppers on page 100 or Turkey Balls with Minty Quinoa on page 230. Many gluten-free grains are now available at supermarkets, but some may also be found at your local health-food store.

weight loss

Gluten-free in itself is not a way to lose weight (because you can still eat sugar), so it's important to ensure your diet is still balanced – eating good protein at every meal, with fresh vegetables, salad and fruits as accompaniments. Shop-bought gluten-free foods may contain more sugar to give them extra taste and texture so, again, cooking from scratch enables you to be in control of what you eat and makes it easier to be aware of how much sugar and calories you consume each day. Portion control is also important, and in this book a calorie intake is given for each recipe to help you to make great-tasting dishes from under 200 to under 500 calories per serving. If you include snacks in your daily intake, just be sure they are healthy choices!

When you are trying to lose weight, the key is to make conscious choices about eating whole, nutritious foods, with a diet that suits your lifestyle, and including exercise to balance what you eat.

recipes under 200 calories

caprese salad

Calories per serving **130**
Serves **4**
Preparation time **10 minutes**

4 large, ripe **beef tomatoes**,
   sliced
4 x 125 g (4 oz) **low-fat
   mozzarella balls**, sliced
handful of **basil leaves**
2 tablespoons **balsamic
   vinegar**
2 tablespoons **extra virgin
   olive oil**
pepper

Divide the tomato slices and mozzarella slices between
4 plates, layering them alternately.

Sprinkle with the basil leaves, pepper, vinegar and
olive oil and serve.

For tomato & basil soup, heat 1 tablespoon olive
oil in a pan, add 1 finely chopped onion and fry for
2–3 minutes, then add 1 crushed garlic clove and cook
for a further 1 minute until softened. Add 3 x 400 g
(13 oz) cans chopped tomatoes, 50 g (2 oz) chopped
basil, ½ teaspoon sugar, ½ teaspoon Worcestershire
sauce and 1 tablespoon tomato purée. Mix well, then
pour in 400 ml (14 fl oz) boiling water and mix again.
Bring to the boil, then reduce the heat and simmer for
30 minutes. Using a hand-hand blender, blend the soup
until smooth. Ladle into 4 bowls and serve sprinkled
with pepper, a drizzle of olive oil and a few basil leaves.
Calories per serving 131

cauliflower & peanut salad

Calories per serving **156**
Serves **4**
Preparation time **5 minutes**
Cooking time **5 minutes**

1 **cauliflower**, broken into
   florets
1 teaspoon **mustard seeds**
small bunch of **coriander**,
   chopped
juice of 2 **limes**
½ teaspoon **clear honey**
1 tablespoon **olive oil**
1 tablespoon **black sesame
   seeds**
30 g (1 oz) **gluten-free dry-
   roasted peanuts**, lightly
   crushed

Place the cauliflower in a steamer and steam for
3 minutes until just tender. Place in a serving dish.

Meanwhile, heat a nonstick frying pan and dry-fry the
mustard seeds until they start to pop. Set aside.

Mix together the chopped coriander, lime juice, honey
and olive oil in a small bowl.

Add the dressing, toasted mustard seeds, sesame
seeds and peanuts to the cauliflower and toss together,
then serve.

For spicy cauliflower soup, heat 1 tablespoon
olive oil in a pan, add 1 chopped onion and fry for
2–3 minutes until softened, then add 1 teaspoon
turmeric, 1 teaspoon ground coriander and 1 teaspoon
ground cumin. Stir in the florets of 1 cauliflower and
mix well to coat with all the spices. Pour in 1.5 litres
(2½ pints) hot gluten-free vegetable stock and simmer
for 25–30 minutes until tender. Using a hand-held
blender, blend the soup until smooth. Ladle into
4 bowls and serve sprinkled with 1 tablespoon
chopped coriander. **Calories per serving 143**

onion, tomato & chickpea soup

Calories per serving **150 (not including bread)**
Serves **6**
Preparation time **15 minutes**
Cooking time **1 hour 10 minutes**

2 tablespoons **olive oil**
2 **red onions**, roughly chopped
2 **garlic cloves**, finely chopped
2 teaspoons **brown sugar**
625 g (1¼ lb) **tomatoes**, skinned if liked, roughly chopped
2 teaspoons **harissa paste**
3 teaspoons **tomato purée**
400 g (13 oz) can **chickpeas**, rinsed and drained
900 ml (1½ pints) **gluten-free vegetable** or **chicken stock**
salt and **pepper**

Heat the oil in a large saucepan, add the onions and fry over a low heat for 10 minutes, stirring occasionally, until just beginning to brown around the edges. Stir in the garlic and sugar and cook for a further 10 minutes, stirring more frequently as the onions begin to caramelize.

Stir in the tomatoes and harissa paste and fry for 5 minutes. Mix in the tomato purée, chickpeas, stock and salt and pepper and bring to the boil. Cover, reduce the heat and simmer for 45 minutes until the tomatoes and onion are very soft. Taste and adjust the seasoning if needed.

Ladle into 6 bowls and serve with warm gluten-free tomato ciabatta, if liked.

For chillied red onion & bean soup, make the soup as above but omit the harissa and add 1 teaspoon smoked paprika and 1 split dried red chilli when frying the tomatoes. Replace the chickpeas with a rinsed and drained 400 g (13 oz) can red kidney beans. Serve with gluten-free garlic bread, if liked. **Calories per serving 144 (not including bread)**

minted spring lamb soup

Calories per serving **199**
Serves **4**
Preparation time **5 minutes**
Cooking time **10 minutes**

1.8 litres (3 pints) **gluten-free vegetable stock**
150 g (5 oz) **baby carrots**, peeled and sliced
275 g (9 oz) **cooked lamb**, shredded
150 g (5 oz) **peas**
8 **spring onions**, sliced
4 tablespoons chopped **mint**
salt and **pepper**

Pour the stock into a saucepan and bring to a simmer. Add the carrots and cook for 3–4 minutes, then add the lamb and peas and cook for a further 2 minutes until the vegetables are tender.

Stir in the spring onions and mint, then season to taste.

Ladle the soup into 4 bowls and serve.

For minted spring lamb salad, whisk together 2 tablespoons olive oil, 1 tablespoon chopped mint, 2 teaspoons lemon juice, ½ teaspoon clear honey and salt and pepper in a bowl. Place 50g (2 oz) baby spinach leaves, 50 g (2 oz) watercress and 2 sliced roasted peppers in a salad bowl with the seeds of 1 pomegranate, 75 g (3 oz) crumbled feta cheese and 300 g (10 oz) shredded cooked lamb. Toss with the dressing and serve. **Calories per serving 357**

bloody mary soup

Calories per serving **151**
Serves **6**
Preparation time **20 minutes, plus chilling**
Cooking time **25 minutes**

1 tablespoon **olive oil**, plus
    extra to serve
1 **onion**, chopped
1 **red pepper**, cored,
    deseeded and diced
2 **celery sticks**, sliced
500 g (1 lb) **plum tomatoes**,
    chopped
900 ml (1 ½ pints) **gluten-free
    vegetable stock**
2 teaspoons **caster sugar**
4 teaspoons **Worcestershire
    sauce**
4 teaspoons **tomato purée**
4 tablespoons **vodka**
few drops of **Tabasco sauce**
salt and **pepper**
baby celery sticks with leaves,
    to garnish

Heat the oil in a saucepan, add the onion and fry for 5 minutes until softened but not browned. Stir in the red pepper, celery and tomatoes and fry for 5 minutes, stirring occasionally.

Pour in the stock, add the sugar, Worcestershire sauce, tomato purée and a little salt and pepper and bring to the boil. Cover and simmer for 15 minutes.

Leave the soup to cool slightly, then purée in batches in a blender or food processor until smooth. Sieve, if liked, then pour back into the saucepan. Add the vodka and Tabasco to taste, and adjust the seasoning if needed. Chill well.

Ladle the soup into 6 small glasses or bowls, add tiny celery sticks, drizzle with a little extra olive oil and sprinkle with a little extra pepper.

For Virgin Mary & pesto soup, fry the onion in the oil as above, add the red pepper, celery and tomatoes, then simmer in 900 ml (1 ½ pints) gluten-free stock mixed with 4 teaspoons sun-dried tomato paste and 2 teaspoons caster sugar for 15 minutes. Purée with 1 tablespoon pesto. Chill and serve with a little extra pesto added to each bowl and garnished with a few tiny basil leaves. **Calories per serving 154**

smoked haddock & kale soup

Calories per serving **198**
Serves **4**
Preparation time **10 minutes**
Cooking time **20–25 minutes**

1 tablespoon **olive oil**
2 **shallots**, diced
3 **garlic cloves**, crushed
1 **large potato**, peeled and
   diced
350 ml (12 fl oz)
   unsweetened soya milk
500 ml (17 fl oz) **water**
300 g (10 oz) **kale**, shredded
300 g (10 oz) **smoked
   haddock**, skinned and
   chopped
salt and **pepper**

Heat the oil in a saucepan, add the shallots and garlic and cook for 3–4 minutes until softened. Add the potato, milk and measurement water and season to taste. Bring to the boil, then reduce the heat and simmer for 5–6 minutes.

Stir in the kale and cook for a further 10–12 minutes until the vegetables are tender. Stir in the haddock and simmer for 2 minutes, or until cooked through.

Ladle the soup into 4 bowls and serve immediately.

For smoked haddock fishcakes with kale, cook 400 g (13 oz) smoked haddock under a preheated hot grill for 4 minutes on each side, then skin and flake into a large bowl. Mix in 625 g (1¼ lb) mashed potatoes, 1 tablespoon chopped rinsed and drained capers, the grated rind of 1 lemon, 2 tablespoons chopped parsley and 1 beaten egg. Mix well, then shape into 8 fishcakes and dust with a little flour. Heat 2 tablespoons olive oil in a frying pan and cook the fishcakes for 3–4 minutes on each side until golden. Meanwhile, heat 2 tablespoons olive oil in a separate pan, add 250 g (8 oz) chopped kale and cook for 3–4 minutes until wilted. Serve with the fishcakes. **Calories per serving 297**

asparagus with poached eggs

Calories per serving **199**
Serves **4**
Preparation time **5 minutes**
Cooking time **6–8 minutes**

4 **eggs**
700 g (1½ lb) **asparagus spears**
1 tablespoon **olive oil**
40 g (1½ oz) **Parmesan cheese** shavings

Bring a saucepan of water to a gentle simmer and stir with a large spoon to create a swirl. Break 2 eggs into the water and cook for 3–4 minutes. Remove with a slotted spoon and keep warm. Repeat with the remaining eggs.

Meanwhile, snap the woody ends off the asparagus spears and discard. Heat a griddle pan until very hot and sprinkle it with the oil, then add the asparagus and cook, turning frequently, until slightly charred and just tender.

Divide the asparagus on to 4 plates and top with the poached eggs. Sprinkle over the Parmesan shavings and serve.

For asparagus omelette, heat the oil in a frying pan, add 6 trimmed and chopped asparagus spears, 2 sliced spring onions and 3–4 sliced chestnut mushrooms and cook for 5–6 minutes until softened. Whisk together 5 eggs and 4 tablespoons semi-skimmed milk in a jug, then pour into the pan, tipping the pan and moving the egg with a spatula to ensure it cooks evenly. Sprinkle with 25 g (1 oz) grated Parmesan, then place under a preheated hot grill for 1–2 minutes until golden. Cut into quarters and serve with a green salad and new potatoes, if liked. **Calories per serving 222 (not including salad and potatoes)**

veg kebabs with dipping sauce

Calories per serving **192**
Serves **4**
Preparation time **20 minutes**
Cooking time **12–15 minutes**

3 **red onions**, cut into wedges
2 **courgettes**, thickly sliced
2 **red peppers**, cored,
    deseeded and chopped
1 **yellow pepper**, cored,
    deseeded and chopped
3½ tablespoons **olive oil**
1 tablespoon **balsamic**
    vinegar
2 tablespoons chopped **fresh**
    herbs
salt and **pepper**

Thread the vegetables alternately on to 8 bamboo skewers that have been presoaked in water for 10 minutes to prevent burning. Brush the vegetables with ½ tablespoon of the oil and season well with salt and pepper.

Cook the kebabs under a preheated hot grill or on a barbecue for 12–15 minutes, turning frequently, until tender.

Meanwhile, make the dipping sauce. Mix together the remaining oil, vinegar and herbs in a small bowl.

Serve the vegetable kebabs with the dipping sauce.

For quick vegetable & herb soup, heat 1 tablespoon olive oil in a saucepan over a medium heat, add 1 large chopped onion, 2 sliced garlic cloves, 3 sliced celery sticks and 300 g (10 oz) finely diced butternut squash and cook for 2–3 minutes. Pour in a 400 g (13 oz) can chopped tomatoes and 600 ml (1 pint) hot gluten-free vegetable stock and bring to the boil. Simmer for 7–8 minutes, then stir in 2 tablespoons chopped parsley. Season to taste, ladle into 4 bowls and serve.
Calories per serving 120

sushi triangles

Calories per serving **196**
Serves **4**
Preparation time **20 minutes**

380 g (12 oz) cooked **sushi rice**
sushi rice seasoning, to taste
4 sheets of **nori seaweed**
100 g (3½ oz) **smoked salmon**
50 g (2 oz) **cucumber**, very thinly sliced

To serve
gluten-free soy sauce
wasabi

Season the rice to taste with the sushi rice seasoning.

Place 2 of the seaweed sheets on to a board. Spread a quarter of the rice over each, cover with the smoked salmon, then the cucumber. Spoon over the remaining rice, then top with the other seaweed sheets. Press the sushi down well so the layers stick together.

Cut the sushi into 4 triangles and serve with soy sauce and wasabi.

For prawn & roasted pepper sushi, season the rice as above, then layer on to the seaweed sheets with 100 g (3½ oz) cooked peeled prawns, 1 sliced roasted red pepper and 1 stoned, peeled and sliced ripe avocado. Top with the remaining seaweed sheets and continue as above. **Calories per serving 276**

salmon ceviche

Calories per serving **196**
Serves **4**
Preparation time **15 minutes,
  plus marinating**

400 g (13 oz) **fresh skinless
  salmon fillet**, thinly sliced
juice of 6–8 **limes**
4 **spring onions**, finely
  chopped
2 **celery sticks**, finely sliced
1 tablespoon finely chopped
  coriander leaves
100 g (3½ oz) **watercress**, to
  garnish

Place the salmon in a non-metallic bowl and cover
with the lime juice. Cover and leave to marinate in
the refrigerator for 25 minutes.

When ready to serve, drain the salmon, add the spring
onions, celery and coriander and mix well.

Garnish with the watercress and serve.

For hot-smoked salmon salad, blanch 200 g (7 oz)
trimmed asparagus in a saucepan of boiling water
for 1–2 minutes, then drain and refresh under cold
running water. Whisk together 3 tablespoons extra
virgin olive oil, 1 tablespoon lime juice, 1 teaspoon
gluten-free wholegrain mustard, ½ teaspoon clear
honey and 1 deseeded and diced red chilli in a small
bowl. In a large bowl, toss together 400 g (13 oz)
flaked hot-smoked salmon, 4 sliced spring onions,
a small handful of coriander leaves, 100 g (3½ oz)
sliced radishes, 250 g (8 oz) mixed salad leaves,
12 halved baby plum tomatoes, the cooked asparagus
and the salad dressing. Divide between 4 plates and
serve immediately with lime wedges. **Calories per
serving 367**

devilled chicken

Calories per serving **145**
Serves **4**
Preparation time **10 minutes**
Cooking time **16–20 minutes**

8 **boneless, skinless chicken
    thighs**, about 600 g (1¼ lb)
    in total
salad leaves, to serve

Devil sauce
2 tablespoons **gluten-free
    Dijon mustard**
6 drops of **Tabasco sauce**
2 **garlic cloves**, crushed
1 tablespoon **gluten-free soy
    sauce**

Make the devil sauce. Mix together the mustard, Tabasco, garlic and soy sauce in a shallow dish.

Open out the chicken thighs and trim away any fat. Dip the thighs in the devil sauce and coat each piece well.

Heat a large griddle pan or frying pan. Add the chicken pieces flat on the pan and cook for 8–10 minutes on each side until cooked through. Serve hot or cold with salad leaves.

For jerk chicken, mix 3 tablespoons ready-made gluten-free jerk marinade paste with the grated rind and juice of ½ orange and 2 finely chopped garlic cloves. Dip the chicken in this mixture, then cook as above. Serve with a salad. **Calories per serving 148**

spicy turkey burgers with salsa

Calories per serving **185**
Serves **4**
Preparation time **20 minutes**
Cooking time **10–12 minutes**

400 g (13 oz) **minced turkey**
2 cm (¾ inch) piece of **fresh root ginger**, peeled and grated
4 **spring onions**, finely chopped
1 **red chilli**, deseeded and finely chopped
1 **egg yolk**
2 tablespoons chopped **coriander leaves**
4 **Little Gem lettuces**

Salsa
1 **red pepper**, cored, deseeded and diced
100 g (3½ oz) **tomatoes**, diced
1 small **red onion**, finely diced
½ tablespoon chopped **parsley**
½ tablespoon chopped **coriander leaves**
1 tablespoon **red wine vinegar**
½ tablespoon **olive oil**

Mix together the minced turkey, ginger, spring onions, chilli, egg yolk and coriander in a bowl. Using wet hands, shape the mixture into 4 burgers.

Heat a lightly oiled frying pan and cook the burgers for 5–6 minutes on each side until golden and cooked through.

Meanwhile, for the salsa, mix together the red pepper, tomatoes, onion, parsley, coriander, vinegar and oil in a bowl.

Serve the burgers on a bed of lettuce leaves, topped with the salsa.

For Asian turkey salad, mix together 3 finely sliced shallots with ¼ teaspoon salt and leave to stand for 10 minutes. Whisk together the juice of 1 lime, 2 tablespoons gluten-free fish sauce, 1 tablespoon rice vinegar, 1 tablespoon caster sugar, 2 crushed garlic cloves and 1 finely diced red chilli. In a large bowl, toss together 350 g (11½ oz) cooked turkey, cut into strips, 400 g (13 oz) finely shredded Chinese cabbage, 1 large peeled and grated carrot, 100 g (3½ oz) bean sprouts and a small handful each of mint and basil. Toss in the shallots and dressing and leave to stand for 5 minutes, then serve sprinkled with 50 g (2 oz) chopped roasted peanuts. **Calories per serving 149**

vietnamese rice paper rolls

Calories per roll with sauce **57**
Makes **12**
Preparation time **15 minutes**

125 g (4 oz) **cooked peeled prawns**
¼ **cucumber**, cut into matchsticks
handful of **coriander leaves**, chopped
handful of **mint**, chopped
handful of **Thai basil**, chopped
150 g (5 oz) **cold cooked rice vermicelli**
¼ **iceberg lettuce**, shredded
12 **round rice paper sheets**
lime wedges, to serve

Dipping sauce
1 tablespoon **sesame seeds**
2 tablespoons **gluten-free sweet chilli dipping sauce**
juice of 1 **lime**
1 tablespoon **gluten-free Thai fish sauce**

Heat a nonstick frying pan over a medium-low heat and dry-fry the sesame seeds for 2 minutes, stirring frequently, until golden brown and toasted. Set aside.

Mix together the prawns, cucumber, herbs, vermicelli and lettuce in a large bowl.

Soak 1 rice sheet in a bowl of warm water for 20 seconds, then drain on kitchen paper. Fill with the prawn mixture, leaving about 2.5 cm (1 inch) at the top and the bottom of the sheet. Fold over the top and bottom edges and roll up. Repeat with the remaining rice sheets and filling.

Whisk together the remaining dipping sauce ingredients and toasted sesame seeds in a serving dish and serve with the rolls and lime wedges.

For crab rolls, omit the prawns and cucumber and replace with 200 g (7 oz) fresh white crab meat and 4 finely sliced spring onions. Continue as above.
Calories per roll with sauce **67**

smoked salmon sesame blinis

Calories per blini **50**
Makes **25**
Preparation time **10 minutes,**
    plus chilling
Cooking time **10 minutes**

100 g (3½ oz) **gluten-free**
    plain flour
1 **egg**
150 ml (¼ pint) **soya yogurt**
2 tablespoons **cold water**
1 **red chilli**, deseeded and
    chopped
8 **spring onions**, finely sliced
2 tablespoons chopped
    coriander leaves
1 tablespoon **sesame seeds**
1 tablespoon **sunflower oil**
4 tablespoons **low-fat crème**
    fraîche
150 g (5 oz) **smoked salmon**,
    sliced
salt and **pepper**
chopped **chives**, to garnish

Place the flour, egg, yogurt and measurement water in a blender or food processor and process to form a smooth batter. Pour into a bowl, then stir in the chilli, spring onions, coriander, sesame seeds and salt and pepper. Cover and chill for 20 minutes.

Heat a frying pan with a little of the oil and then wipe with kitchen paper. Add dessertspoonfuls of the mixture and cook for 1 minute on each side until lightly golden, then remove from the pan and keep warm. Repeat with the remaining batter.

Top each blini with a little dollop of crème fraîche, a piece of smoked salmon and a sprinkling of chopped chives and sprinkle with a little extra pepper.

For grilled sesame salmon, whisk together 2 tablespoons gluten-free soy sauce, 2 teaspoons clear honey, 2 teaspoons peeled and grated fresh root ginger, 1 tablespoon sesame oil and 2 crushed garlic cloves. Place 4 x 150 g (5 oz) salmon fillets in a shallow bowl and pour over the marinade. Cover and leave to marinate in the refrigerator for 10–15 minutes. Cook the salmon fillets, skin side up, under a preheated grill for 5–6 minutes, then turn the fillets over, sprinkle with 2 tablespoons sesame seeds and cook for a further 3–4 minutes until golden and cooked through. Serve with a crisp green salad. **Calories per serving 351**

carrot & cumin crispbreads

Calories per crispbread **99**
Makes **20**
Preparation time **15 minutes**
Cooking time **30 minutes**

50 g (2 oz) **sunflower seeds**
50 g (2 oz) **pumpkin seeds**
50 g (2 oz) **sesame seeds**
100 g (3½ oz) **whole almonds**, toasted
1½ tablespoons **cumin seeds**
2 **carrots**, peeled and grated
3 tablespoons **pesto**
1 tablespoon **olive oil**, plus extra for greasing
2–3 tablespoons **cold water**

Place the sunflower, pumpkin and sesame seeds, almonds and 1 tablespoon of the cumin seeds in a blender or food processor and pulse until broken down. Add the grated carrots, pesto, oil and measurement water and process until a thick paste forms.

Spread the crispbread mixture over a greased baking sheet to about 5 mm (¼ inch) thick, then score into 20 rectangles and sprinkle over the remaining cumin seeds. Bake in a preheated oven, 200°C (400°F), Gas Mark 6, for 25 minutes until golden and firm.

Cut through the score lines to separate the crispbreads, then turn over and bake for a further 5–6 minutes until crisp and golden. Transfer to a wire rack and leave to cool. Store in an airtight container and eat within 4–5 days.

For carrot & cumin soup, dry-fry 2 teaspoons cumin seeds in a pan, then add 1 tablespoon olive oil, 600 g (1¼ lb) peeled and chopped carrots, 125 g (4 oz) red lentils and 1 litre (1¾ pints) gluten-free vegetable stock and bring to the boil. Reduce the heat and simmer for 15–18 minutes until the carrots are tender and the lentils are swollen and soft. Using a hand-held blender, blend the soup until smooth. Ladle into 4 bowls and serve sprinkled with 2 tablespoons toasted pumpkin seeds and 1 tablespoon chopped parsley. **Calories per serving 251**

chilli corn bread

Calories per square **115**
Makes **16** squares
Preparation time **5 minutes**
Cooking time **30–35 minutes**

3 tablespoons **olive oil**, plus
   extra for greasing
150 g (5 oz) **rice flour**
150 g (5 oz) **polenta**
1 teaspoon **salt**
2 teaspoons **gluten-free
   baking powder**
1 tablespoon **caster sugar**
3 tablespoons grated
   Parmesan cheese
handful of **fresh herbs**,
   chopped
1 **red chilli**, deseeded and
   finely chopped
2 **eggs**, beaten
300 ml (½ pint) **buttermilk**

Grease a 20 cm (8 inch) square cake tin with olive oil.

Sift together the flour, polenta, salt and baking powder into a large bowl. Stir in the sugar, Parmesan, herbs and chilli.

Mix together the oil, eggs and buttermilk in a separate bowl, then pour into the dry ingredients and gently stir until combined.

Pour the mixture into the prepared tin and bake in a preheated oven, 190°C (375°F), Gas Mark 5, for 30–35 minutes until golden. Transfer to a wire rack and leave to cool, then cut into 16 squares. The bread is best eaten on the same day.

For bacon & sweetcorn bread, stir a drained 200 g (7 oz) can sweetcorn and 6 grilled chopped bacon rashers into the dry ingredients and continue as above.
Calories per square 150

carrot & lentil muffins

Calories per muffin **141**
Makes **12**
Preparation time **15 minutes**
Cooking time **25–30 minutes**

75 g (3 oz) **red lentils**
275 ml (9 fl oz) **water**
275 g (9 oz) **gluten-free plain flour**
2 tablespoons **ground flaxseed**
1½ teaspoons **gluten-free baking powder**
50 g (2 oz) **dark muscovado sugar**
1 teaspoon **ground cinnamon**
½ teaspoon **ground cloves**
3 tablespoons **ready-made gluten-free apple sauce**
3 tablespoons **clear honey**
3 tablespoons **sunflower oil**
1 **egg**
1 large **carrot**, peeled and grated
2–3 tablespoons **soya milk** (optional)

Line a 12-hole muffin tin with paper muffin cases.

Place the lentils and measurement water in a saucepan, bring to the boil, then reduce the heat and simmer for 8 minutes until soft. Drain.

Sift the flour, flaxseed and baking powder into a large bowl, then stir in the sugar and spices.

Place the drained lentils in a blender or food processor with the apple sauce, honey, oil and egg and blend until smooth.

Pour the wet ingredients into the dry, stirring in the grated carrots when nearly blended. Add the soya milk to loosen the mixture, if needed.

Spoon the mixture into the muffin cases and bake in a preheated oven, 180°C (350°F), Gas Mark 5, for 18–20 minutes until risen and golden. Transfer to a wire rack and leave to cool.

For carrot & lentil soup, dry-fry 2 teaspoons cumin seeds and a pinch of dried chilli flakes in a small frying pan for 1 minute. Heat 1 tablespoon olive oil in a saucepan, then add half of the spices, 600 g (1¼ lb) peeled and grated carrots, 150 g (5 oz) red lentils, 1 litre (1¾ pints) gluten-free vegetable stock and 125 ml (4 fl oz) milk to the pan and bring to the boil. Simmer for 12–15 minutes until the lentils are soft and swollen. Using a hand-held blender, blend the soup until smooth. Ladle into 4 bowls, drizzle each with 30 g (1 oz) natural yogurt, then serve with a few coriander leaves and the remaining spices sprinkled over the top. **Calories per serving 250**

lemon cookies

Calories per cookie **146**
Makes **20**
Preparation time **20 minutes**
Cooking time **12–15 minutes**

125 ml (4 fl oz) **oil**

4 tablespoons **soya yogurt**

3 **lemons**

125 g (4 oz) **light muscovado sugar**

165 g (5½ oz) **gluten-free plain flour**

75 g (3 oz) **gluten-free rolled oats**

40 g (1½ oz) **millet flakes**

40 g (1½ oz) **desiccated coconut**, plus 1 tablespoon for dusting

Mix together the olive oil, yogurt, juice of 1 lemon and grated rind of 2 lemons in a bowl. In a separate bowl, mix together the sugar, flour, oats, millet and coconut.

Stir the wet ingredients into the dry ingredients and mix to form a soft dough.

Roll the dough into 20 balls, then place on a baking sheet and press down gently. Sprinkle the cookies with the remaining desiccated coconut and the grated rind of 1 lemon.

Bake in a preheated oven, 180°C (350°F), Gas Mark 4, for 12–15 minutes until golden. Leave to cool on the sheet for a few minutes, then transfer to a wire rack and leave to cool completely. Store in an airtight container and eat within 2–3 days.

For lemon posset, mix together 400 g (13 oz) fat-free Greek yogurt, 1 tablespoon icing sugar, the grated rind of 3 lemons and 2 teaspoons lemon juice in a bowl. Spoon into 4 small glasses or bowls and chill for at least 1 hour. Sprinkle 1 tablespoon desiccated coconut over the possets, then serve each with 1 lemon cookie (see above). **Calories per serving 238**

orange shortbread cookies

Calories per cookie **59**
Makes **10**
Preparation time **10 minutes,
plus chilling**
Cooking time **12–15 minutes**

100 g (3½ oz) **unsalted
butter**, softened, plus extra
for greasing
50 g (2 oz) **caster sugar**
grated rind of 1 **orange**
175 g (6 oz) **gluten-free plain
flour**
½ teaspoon **gluten-free
baking powder**

Beat the butter in a bowl until soft, then cream together
with the sugar and orange rind until light and fluffy.
Stir in the flour and baking powder and mix to form a
light dough.

Roll the dough into a circle about 5 mm (¼ inch) thick
and frill the edge with the back of a fork. Cut into
10 wedges and place on a greased baking sheet. Chill
for 15 minutes.

Bake in a preheated oven, 190°C (375°F), Gas Mark
5, for 12–15 minutes until golden. Leave to cool on
the baking sheet for 2 minutes, then transfer to a wire
rack and leave to cool completely. Store in an airtight
container and eat within 3–4 days.

For amaretti orange dessert, divide 10 crumbled
gluten-free amaretti biscuits between 4 glasses or
small bowls. Stir the grated rind of 4 oranges into
400 g (13 oz) fat-free Greek yogurt. Segment the
4 grated oranges over a bowl to catch the juice, then
place the orange segments on top of the crushed
biscuits and pour over any juice. Top with the yogurt
and sprinkle each one with 1 teaspoon muscovado
sugar. Chill for 20 minutes before serving. **Calories
per serving 204**

balsamic strawberries & mango

Calories per serving **109**
Serves **4**
Preparation time **5 minutes,**
   plus overnight chilling and
   standing

500 g (1 lb) **strawberries,**
   hulled and thickly sliced
1 large **mango,** peeled, stoned
   and sliced
1–2 tablespoons **caster sugar**
3 tablespoons **balsamic**
   vinegar
2 tablespoons chopped **mint,**
   to decorate

Mix together the strawberries and mango in a large,
shallow non-metallic bowl, sprinkle with the sugar,
according to taste, and pour over the vinegar. Cover
with clingfilm and chill overnight.

Remove the fruit from the refrigerator and leave
to stand for at least 1 hour before serving.

Spoon the fruit into 4 serving bowls, drizzle over the
syrup and serve sprinkled with the mint.

For peppery strawberries & blueberries, mix the
strawberries with 125 g (4 oz) blueberries and make
as above. Sprinkle with a few grinds of pepper and the
chopped mint before serving. **Calories per serving 83**

chocolate orange mousse

Calories per serving **189**
Serves **4**
Preparation time **15 minutes,
    plus cooling and chilling**
Cooking time **5 minutes**

80 g (3 oz) **gluten-free plain
    dark chocolate**, chopped
1 tablespoon **gluten-free
    cocoa powder**
½ teaspoon **gluten-free
    coffee granules**
grated rind of **1 orange**
2 tablespoons **water**
2 **egg whites**
1 tablespoon **caster sugar**
50 g (2 oz) **fat-free Greek
    yogurt**
raspberries, to serve

Melt the chocolate in a bowl set over a pan of gently simmering water, making sure the bottom of the bowl does not touch the water. Stir occasionally, then leave to cool.

Mix together the cocoa powder, coffee, orange rind and measurement water in a small bowl, then add to the chocolate.

Whisk the egg whites in a clean bowl until they form soft peaks, then add the sugar and continue to whisk until thick and glossy.

Stir the yogurt into the cooled chocolate mixture, then fold in a quarter of the egg whites. Gently fold in the remaining whites until evenly mixed.

Spoon into 4 ramekins or glasses and chill for 2 hours before serving, topped with raspberries.

For homemade chocolate orange, grate the rind from 1 orange and reserve. Cut the orange in half, scoop out the flesh and discard, then line the halves with clingfilm. Melt 200 g (7 oz) gluten-free plain dark chocolate, 20 g (¾ oz) unsalted butter and the reserved orange rind in a heatproof bowl set over a pan of gently simmering water. Pour the chocolate mixture into the orange halves and leave to set in a cool place for a few hours. Using the clingfilm, lift out the chocolate halves, peel off the clingfilm and cut into 10 wedges to serve. **Calories per wedge 129**

elderflower poached pears

Calories per serving **191**
Serves **4**
Preparation time **5 minutes,**
  plus cooling
Cooking time **25 minutes**

125 ml (4 fl oz) **elderflower**
  and pear or **elderflower and**
  apple cordial
500 ml (17 fl oz) **apple juice**
2 teaspoons **lemon juice**
4 large **pears**, peeled, cored
  and quartered
pinch of **saffron** threads

Mix the cordial, apple juice and lemon juice in a small, deep saucepan. Bring to a gentle simmer and add the pears and saffron. Simmer gently for about 25 minutes or until the pears are tender.

Remove from the heat, cover and leave to cool completely in the poaching liquid. Carefully remove the pears with a slotted spoon and divide into 4 serving bowls. Ladle over the poaching liquid to serve.

For baked apples in elderflower & saffron, replace the pears with 4 peeled, cored and quartered apples and place in a deep ovenproof dish. Heat the cordial, apple juice and saffron as above, omitting the lemon juice, and pour over the apples. Cover with foil and place in a preheated oven, 180°C (350 °C), Gas Mark 4, for about 1 hour or until the apples are tender. **Calories per serving 175**

mango & passion fruit roulade

Calories per serving **199**

Serves **6**

Preparation time **20 minutes,
plus standing**

Cooking time **30 minutes**

3 large **egg whites**

175 g (6 oz) **caster sugar**

1 teaspoon **cornflour**

1 teaspoon **white wine
vinegar**

3 tablespoon **icing sugar**

200 g (7 oz) **fat-free Greek
yogurt**

1 large ripe **mango**, peeled,
stoned and diced

4 **passion fruits**, pulp only

Line a 23 cm x 33 cm (9 inch x 13 inch) Swiss roll tin
with nonstick baking paper.

Whisk the egg whites in a large clean bowl until frothy
and doubled in size. Add the sugar a spoonful at a
time and continue to whisk until thick and glossy.
Mix together the cornflour and vinegar in a small bowl,
then whisk into the meringue mixture. Spoon into the
prepared tin and gently level the surface.

Bake in a preheated oven, 150°C (300°F), Gas
Mark 2, for 30 minutes until the meringue is just firm.
Remove from the oven and cover with a sheet of damp
greaseproof paper for 6–8 minutes.

Dust another sheet of greaseproof paper with icing
sugar and turn the meringue out on to it, discarding
the damp sheet. Peel off the lining paper.

Spread the yogurt over the meringue, then sprinkle
over the mango and passion fruit pulp.

Using the paper to help, roll up the roulade from one
short end. Transfer to a serving plate, seam down, and
sift a little icing sugar over to serve.

For mango & passion fruit brûlée, divide 1 large
ripe peeled, stoned and diced mango and the pulp of
4 passion fruits between 6 ramekins. Top each one
with 2 tablespoons fat-free Greek yogurt and sprinkle
with ½ tablespoon dark muscovado sugar. Chill for
15 minutes before serving. **Calories per serving 113**

instant summer berry sorbet

Calories per serving **178**
Serves **4**
Preparation time **10 minutes**

300 g (10 oz) **frozen summer berries**
400 ml (14 fl oz) **raspberry yogurt**
6 tablespoons **icing sugar**

Tip the frozen berries, yogurt and icing sugar into a food processor or blender. Whizz until blended. Scrape the mixture from the sides and blend again.

Spoon the sorbet into 4 chilled glasses or bowls and serve immediately.

For frozen berries with white & dark hot chocolate sauce, divide 400 g (13 oz) frozen mixed berries between 4 chilled serving plates or shallow bowls. Melt 75 g (3 oz) gluten-free plain dark chocolate and 75 g (3 oz) gluten-free white chocolate in 2 separate small pans. Whip 150 ml (¼ pint) double cream until soft peaks form. When ready to serve, drizzle the hot chocolate sauces over the frozen berries and serve immediately with a dollop of the whipped cream. Calories per serving 496

recipes under 300 calories

pear & stilton salad

Calories per serving **295**
Serves **4**
Preparation time **15 minutes**

100 g (3½ oz) **watercress**
2 **heads of chicory**, sliced
3 **pears**, cored and sliced
¼ **cucumber**, sliced
juice of **1 lemon**
½ teaspoon **clear honey**
½ teaspoon **gluten-free wholegrain mustard**
2 tablespoons **extra virgin olive oil**
100 g (3½ oz) **Stilton cheese**, rind removed and crumbled
2 tablespoons **chopped walnuts**

Toss together the watercress, chicory, pears and cucumber and place on a serving plate or in a large salad bowl.

Whisk together the lemon juice, honey, mustard and olive oil in a small bowl, then drizzle over the leaves. Sprinkle over the Stilton and walnuts and serve.

For Stilton & pear soup, melt 15 g (½ oz) butter in a pan, add 1 chopped onion and fry for 2–3 minutes until softened. Add 4 peeled, cored and chopped pears and 850 ml (1½ pints) gluten-free vegetable stock and bring to the boil, then reduce the heat and simmer for 15–18 minutes until the pears are tender. Using a hand-held blender, blend the soup until smooth. Return to the heat and crumble in 125 g (4 oz) Stilton cheese and stir until it melts. Add a squeeze of lemon juice and season to taste. Serve sprinkled with 1 tablespoon chopped chives. **Calories per serving 268**

beef carpaccio & bean salad

Calories per serving **275**
Serves **4**
Preparation time **15 minutes,
  plus freezing**
Cooking time **2–3 minutes**

250 g (8 oz) **beef fillet**
3 tablespoons **extra virgin
  olive oil**
1 teaspoon **pepper**
1 tablespoon chopped **thyme
  leaves**
1 teaspoon **gluten-free Dijon
  mustard**
½ tablespoon **balsamic
  vinegar**
½ teaspoon **clear honey**
125 g (4 oz) **green beans**,
  trimmed
400 g (13 oz) can **cannellini
  beans**, rinsed and drained
1 small **red onion**, thinly sliced
25g (1 oz) **Parmesan cheese**
  shavings, to garnish

Place the beef fillet on a chopping board and rub with
1 tablespoon of the oil, the pepper and thyme. Wrap
in clingfilm and place in the freezer for 20 minutes.

Meanwhile, whisk together the remaining oil with the
mustard, vinegar and honey in a bowl.

Blanch the green beans for 2–3 minutes in boiling
water, then refresh under cold running water. Toss the
green beans, cannellini beans and sliced onion in the
dressing and leave to stand at room temperature.

Unwrap the beef fillet, slice as thinly as possible
and arrange on a serving plate. Spoon over the bean
salad, with all the dressing, and garnish with shavings
of Parmesan.

For nutty beef & bean salad, rub 450 g (14½ oz)
rump steak with 1 tablespoon olive oil and sprinkle with
1 tablespoon pepper. Fry the steak for 1–2 minutes
on each side in 1 tablespoon olive oil, then leave to
rest. In a large bowl, toss together 40 g (1½ oz) lamb's
lettuce, 2 chopped ready-cooked fresh beetroots, 4 sliced
spring onions, a rinsed and drained 400 g (13 oz)
can butter beans, 12 halved baby plum tomatoes and
2 tablespoons toasted cashew nuts. Whisk together
3 tablespoons extra virgin olive oil, 1 tablespoon
balsamic vinegar, 1 crushed garlic clove,1 teaspoon
soft dark brown sugar and ½ teaspoon gluten-free
wholegrain mustard in a bowl, then stir in 1 tablespoon
roughly chopped peanuts. Slice the steak and place on
top of the salad, then pour over the dressing to serve.
Calories per serving 460

peach, feta & watercress salad

Calories per serving **259**
Serves **4**
Preparation time **10 minutes**
Cooking time **2–3 minutes**

30 g (1 oz) **pumpkin seeds**
juice of ½ **lemon**
2 tablespoons **extra virgin
olive oil**
½ teaspoon **gluten-free Dijon
mustard**
1 teaspoon **clear honey**
1 tablespoon chopped
oregano
75 g (3 oz) **watercress**
3 **peaches**, halved, stoned and
sliced
4 **spring onions**, sliced
175 g (6 oz) **feta cheese**,
crumbled
pepper

Heat a nonstick frying pan over a medium-low heat and dry-fry the pumpkin seeds for 2–3 minutes, stirring frequently, until slightly golden and toasted. Set aside.

Whisk together the lemon juice, oil, mustard, honey, oregano and pepper in a small bowl.

Divide the watercress between 4 plates, top with the peach slices and spring onions, then sprinkle over the feta cheese.

Serve sprinkled with the toasted pumpkin seeds and drizzled with the dressing.

For peach, feta & watercress bruschetta, cut 2 gluten-free baguettes into 1.5 cm (¾ inch) slices. Place the slices on a baking sheet and drizzle with 2 tablespoons olive oil. Bake in a preheated oven, 200°C (400°F), Gas Mark 6, for 10–12 minutes until golden. Rub one side of each slice with a garlic clove. Halve, stone and slice 4 peaches. Top the toasts with a few watercress sprigs, the peach slices and 125 g (4 oz) crumbled feta cheese. Serve drizzled with balsamic glaze. **Calories per serving 384**

monkfish kebabs with tabbouleh

Calories per serving **285**
Serves **4**
Preparation time **20 minutes,**
   plus marinating
Cooking time **25–30 minutes**

3.5 cm (1 ½ inch) piece of
   fresh root ginger, peeled
   and diced
grated rind and juice of 1
   lemon
½ teaspoon **turmeric**
2 **garlic cloves,** crushed
½ teaspoon **dried chilli flakes**
1 tablespoon chopped **mint**
4 tablespoons **natural yogurt**
500 g (1 lb) **monkfish,**
   skinned and cut into
   bite-sized chunks
200 g (7 oz) **quinoa**
4 tablespoons chopped
   parsley
2 tablespoons chopped
   coriander leaves
50 g (2 oz) **cherry tomatoes,**
   quartered
lemon wedges, to serve

Mix together the ginger, lemon rind and juice, turmeric, garlic, chilli flakes, half the mint and the yogurt in a small bowl.

Thread the monkfish on to 8 bamboo skewers that have been presoaked in water for 10 minutes to prevent burning, then place in a shallow non-metallic dish. Pour over the yogurt marinade and leave to marinate for 20 minutes.

Meanwhile, cook the quinoa in a saucepan of boiling water according to the packet instructions, then drain and refresh under cold running water and drain again. Transfer to a bowl and stir in the remaining mint, the parsley, coriander and tomatoes.

Cook the kebabs under a preheated hot grill or on a barbecue for 10–12 minutes, turning frequently, until the fish is cooked through. Serve with the tabbouleh and lemon wedges.

For monkfish & mango salad, toss together 400 g (13 oz) monkfish, cut into chunks, 2 tablespoons olive oil and 1 tablespoon red Thai curry paste in a bowl and leave to marinate for 20 minutes. Meanwhile, toss together the leaves of 2 Little Gem lettuces, 1 peeled, stoned and sliced mango, ¼ sliced cucumber, a small bunch of chopped coriander and 3 sliced spring onions, then then transfer to a large serving plate. Heat a frying pan (or you can cook over a barbecue) and cook the monkfish for 2–3 minutes on each side until cooked through. Spoon on to the salad and serve sprinkled with 1 tablespoon toasted almond flakes, a squeeze of lime juice and a drizzle of olive oil. **Calories per serving 234**

butternut & cumin soup

Calories per serving **221**
Serves **4**
Preparation time **10 minutes**
Cooking time **40–45 minutes**

2 tablespoons **pumpkin seeds**
1 kg (2 lb) **butternut squash**, peeled, deseeded and chopped
1½ tablespoons **olive oil**
1 teaspoon **dried chilli flakes**
2 teaspoons **cumin seeds**
1 **onion**, chopped
1 **garlic clove**, chopped
600 ml (1 pint) hot **gluten-free vegetable stock**
2 tablespoons **natural yogurt**

Heat a nonstick frying pan over a medium-low heat and dry-fry the pumpkin seeds for 2–3 minutes, stirring frequently, until slightly golden and toasted. Set aside.

Place the squash in a roasting tin, drizzle with 1 tablespoon of the oil and sprinkle with the chilli flakes and cumin seeds. Roast in a preheated oven, 200°C (400°F), Gas Mark 6, for 30–35 minutes until tender, tossing occasionally.

Heat the remaining oil in a saucepan, add the onion and garlic and fry for 3–4 minutes. Add the squash and stock and simmer for 5 minutes. Using a hand-held blender, blend the soup until smooth, adding more liquid to loosen, if necessary.

Ladle the soup into 4 bowls and serve topped with dollops of the yogurt and the toasted pumpkin seeds.

For roasted butternut & cumin salad, place the butternut squash, cut into wedges, in a roasting tin and add the oil and cumin seeds, omitting the chilli flakes. Roast as above. Toss the roasted squash with 75 g (3 oz) watercress, 12 halved cherry tomatoes, 50 g (2 oz) sugar snap peas and 1 cored, deseeded and sliced red pepper in a serving bowl. Drizzle with 2 tablespoons gluten-free low-fat dressing and serve. **Calories per serving 172**

caribbean pepper pot soup

Calories per serving **279**
Serves **6**
Preparation time **20 minutes**
Cooking time **45–50 minutes**

2 tablespoons **olive oil**
1 **onion**, finely chopped
1 **Scotch bonnet chilli**,
  deseeded and finely
  chopped, or 2 **hot Thai red
  chillies**, chopped with seeds
2 **red peppers**, cored,
  deseeded and diced
2 **garlic cloves**, finely chopped
1 large **carrot**, peeled and
  diced
200 g (7 oz) **potatoes**, peeled
  and diced
1 **bay leaf**
1 **thyme sprig**
400 ml (14 fl oz) can **coconut
  milk**
600 ml (1 pint) **gluten-free
  beef stock**
salt and **cayenne pepper**

To serve
200 g (7 oz) **rump steak**
2 teaspoons **olive oil**

Heat the oil in a saucepan, add the onion and fry gently
for 5 minutes until softened and just beginning to
turn golden. Stir in the chilli, red peppers, garlic, carrot,
potatoes and herbs and fry for 5 minutes, stirring.

Pour in the coconut milk and stock, then season with
salt and cayenne pepper. Bring to the boil, stirring, then
reduce the heat, cover and simmer for 30 minutes, or
until the vegetables are tender. Discard the herbs, then
taste and adjust the seasoning if needed.

Rub the steak with the oil, then season lightly with salt
and cayenne pepper. Heat a griddle or frying pan and
when hot add the steak and fry for 2–5 minutes on
each side until cooked to your liking. Leave to stand
for 5 minutes, then slice thinly.

Ladle the soup into 6 bowls and top with the steak slices.

For prawn & spinach pepper pot soup, make the
soup as above using 600 ml (1 pint) gluten-free fish
stock in place of the beef stock. Simmer for 30 minutes,
then add 200 g (7 oz) raw peeled prawns, defrosted if
frozen, and 125 g (4 oz) spinach. Cook for 3–4 minutes
until the prawns turn pink and are cooked through and
the spinach is just wilted. **Calories per serving 271**

prawns with spicy dip

Calories per serving **227**
Serves **4**
Preparation time **10 minutes**

2 Little Gem lettuces, leaves
  separated
400 g (13 oz) **cooked peeled
  king prawns**

Spicy dip
200 g (7 oz) **cream cheese**
100 g (3½ oz) **natural yogurt**
1 **garlic clove**, crushed
2–3 drops of **lemon juice**
¼ teaspoon **dried chilli flakes**
handful of snipped **chives**
salt and **pepper**

Make the spicy dip. Mix together the cream cheese, yogurt, garlic, lemon juice, chilli flakes and chives in a serving bowl. Season with salt and pepper to taste.

Arrange the lettuce leaves on 4 small plates and top with the prawns. Serve the dip for everyone to share.

For spicy prawn salad, heat 2 tablespoons olive oil in a saucepan, add 1 tablespoon dried chilli flakes and 2 crushed garlic cloves and cook for 2 minutes. Add 500 g (1 lb) raw peeled king prawns and cook for a further 5–6 minutes until the prawns turn pink and are cooked through. Add a splash of white wine and cook until it has evaporated. Remove from the heat. Toss 75 g (3 oz) rocket leaves in 2 tablespoons olive oil and 1 tablespoon balsamic vinegar. Divide between 4 plates and top with 2 peeled, stoned and sliced avocados. Spoon over the prawns and serve sprinkled with 1 tablespoon toasted sesame seeds.
Calories per serving 385

onion bhajis

Calories per serving **213 (not including mango chutney)**
Serves **4**
Preparation time **10 minutes**
Cooking time **10 minutes**

60 g (2¼ oz) **gram flour**
30 g (1 oz) **rice flour**
1 tablespoon melted **butter**
juice of ½ **lemon**
1 teaspoon **cumin seeds**
½ teaspoon **fennel seeds**
½ teaspoon **dried chilli flakes**
½ teaspoon **turmeric**
2 **garlic cloves**, chopped
small bunch of **coriander**, chopped
2 cm (¾ inch) piece of **fresh root ginger**, peeled and grated
2 **onions**, thinly sliced
1 litre (1¾ pints) **sunflower** or **vegetable oil**
salt and **pepper**

Sift the flours into a bowl, then stir in the butter and lemon juice. Add enough cold water to make a batter the consistency of double cream. Stir in all the remaining ingredients except the oil, season and mix well.

Heat the oil in a deep pan to 180–190°C (350–375°F), or until a drop of batter sizzles in the hot oil. Using 2 tablespoons, gently spoon an eighth of the mixture into the oil, then repeat until there are 3 or 4 dollops – try not to overcrowd the pan. Cook for 4–5 minutes, turning occasionally, until crisp and golden. Drain on kitchen paper and keep warm. Repeat with the remaining batter to make 8 bhajis.

Serve with gluten-free mango chutney, if liked.

For onion soup, heat 1 tablespoon olive oil in a frying pan, add 2 crushed garlic cloves and cook for 1 minute. Add 2 diced onions and ½ teaspoon paprika and cook for 5 minutes until softened, then stir in 900 ml (1½ pints) gluten-free chicken stock and bring to the boil. Reduce the heat and simmer for about 30 minutes. Meanwhile, poach 4 eggs (see page 32). Season the soup to taste and ladle into 4 bowls. Top each with a poached egg and coriander sprig. **Calories per serving 165**

roasted peppers

Calories per serving **211**
Serves **4**
Preparation time **10 minutes**
Cooking time **25 minutes**

2 **red peppers**, halved, cored
and deseeded

2 **yellow peppers**, halved,
cored and deseeded

1 small **red onion**, cut into 8
wedges

2 **runner beans**, trimmed and
cut into small batons

1 **courgette**, halved and sliced

3 **garlic cloves**, sliced

2 tablespoons **extra virgin
olive oil**

1 teaspoon **cumin seeds**

120 g (4 oz) **feta** or **goats'
cheese**

salt and **pepper**

Place the pepper halves in a roasting tin and divide the other vegetables and the garlic between them.

Sprinkle with the oil and cumin seeds, season with salt and pepper and bake in a preheated oven, 200°C (400°F), Gas Mark 6, for 25 minutes until tender. Crumble over the cheese and serve.

For red pepper hummus, place a rinsed and drained 400 g (13 oz) can chickpeas in a blender or food processor and add the juice of ½ lemon, 2 crushed garlic cloves, 1 teaspoon ground cumin, 2 drained roasted red peppers from a jar, 2 tablespoons tahini paste and 2–3 tablespoons olive oil. Blend until smooth, adding a little more olive oil if you want to loosen the texture. Serve the hummus with vegetable crudités. **Calories per serving 310**

guacamole

Calories per serving **207 (not including oatcakes or vegetable crudités)**

Serves **4**

Preparation time **10 minutes**

2 **avocados**, peeled, stoned and chopped

juice of **1 lime**

6 **cherry tomatoes**, diced

1 tablespoon chopped **coriander leaves**

1–2 **garlic cloves**, crushed

gluten-free oatcakes or vegetable crudités, such as **cucumber**, **peppers** and **carrots**, to serve

Put the avocados and lime juice in a bowl and mash together to prevent discoloration, then stir in the remaining ingredients.

Serve immediately with gluten-free oatcakes or vegetable crudités, if liked.

For prawn & avocado salad, soak 200 g (7 oz) vermicelli rice noodles in boiling water until just tender. Drain, refresh under cold running water and drain again, then place in a bowl with 200 g (7 oz) cooked peeled king prawns, 2 peeled, stoned and sliced avocados, ½ thinly sliced cucumber and 4 sliced spring onions. Whisk together 100 ml (3½ fl oz) coconut milk, the juice of 1 lime and a 2 cm (¾ inch) piece of fresh root ginger, peeled and grated, in a separate bowl. Pour over the salad and gently toss together to serve. **Calories per serving 445**

trout & dill fishcakes

Calories per serving **286**
Serves **4**
Preparation time **15 minutes,
plus chilling**
Cooking time **25–30 minutes**

300 g (10 oz) **trout fillets**
400 g (13 oz) **mashed
potatoes**
5 **spring onions**, finely
chopped
2 tablespoons **capers**,
chopped
10 g (⅓ oz) **dill**, chopped
grated rind and juice of 1
lemon
1 tablespoon **olive oil**
salt and **pepper**

To serve
steamed **tenderstem broccoli**
lime wedges

Cook the trout fillets under a preheated hot grill for
4 minutes on each side until cooked through, then
discard the skin, break the flesh into flakes and place
in a bowl.

Add the mashed potatoes, spring onions, capers, dill,
lemon rind and 2 tablespoons of lemon juice. Season
with salt and pepper. Shape into 8 cakes and chill for
20 minutes.

Heat the oil in a frying pan and cook the fishcakes, in
batches, for 4–5 minutes on each side or until golden
and cooked through. Serve with steamed tenderstem
broccoli and lime wedges.

For trout & dill pâté, mix together 2 x 150 g (5 oz)
cooked and flaked trout fillets, 1 teaspoon gluten-free
Dijon mustard, 1 tablespoon chopped dill, 300 g (10 oz)
low-fat cream cheese and a pinch of paprika in a bowl.
Season to taste. Spoon into 4 ramekins and chill for
30 minutes. Serve with vegetable crudités. **Calories
per serving 230**

smoked salmon scrambled eggs

Calories per serving **233 (not including toast)**
Serves **4**
Preparation time **5 minutes**
Cooking time **5 minutes**

8 eggs
2 tablespoons **fromage frais**
1 tablespoon chopped **chives**
125 g (4 oz) **smoked salmon**, cut into strips
salt and **pepper**

Whisk together the eggs, fromage frais and salt and pepper in a bowl.

Heat a saucepan over a medium heat, pour in the egg mixture and cook for 1 minute, then using a spatula, gently push the egg around to ensure it cooks evenly.

When the egg looks like creamy curds, stir in the chives and smoked salmon and serve immediately on buttered gluten-free toast, if liked.

For smoked salmon frittata, thickly slice 500 g (1 lb) new potatoes and cook in a pan of boiling water for 8–10 minutes. Drain. Lightly beat 8 large eggs, then stir in 200 g (7 oz) strips of smoked salmon, 2 tablespoons chopped dill, 100 g (3½ oz) petits pois and the potatoes. Season. Heat 2 tablespoons olive oil in a frying pan with an ovenproof handle. Pour in the egg mixture and cook for 10–15 minutes over a low heat until the egg is starting to set. Place under a preheated medium grill and cook for 3–4 minutes, or until the egg is set and the top is golden. Turn out on to a board and cut into wedges to serve. **Calories per serving 393**

spanish-style seafood

Calories per serving **214 (not including bread)**
Serves **4**
Preparation time **15 minutes**
Cooking time **35–40 minutes**

1 tablespoon **olive oil**
2 **garlic cloves**, sliced
1 **fennel bulb**, sliced
500 g (1 lb) **cherry tomatoes**
3 tablespoons **sherry**
1 tablespoon **sun-dried tomato paste**
16 large **live mussels**, scrubbed and debearded (discard any that don't shut when tapped)
16 large **raw peeled prawns**
200 g (7 oz) **squid**, cleaned and cut into slices
small bunch of **parsley**, chopped
salt and **pepper**

Heat the oil in a large shallow frying pan, add the garlic and fennel and cook for 8–10 minutes until softened. Add the tomatoes, sherry, tomato paste and 3 tablespoons of water and bring to the boil, then reduce the heat and simmer for 20 minutes.

Add the mussels, cover with a lid and cook for 5–6 minutes until the mussels have opened. Discard any that remain closed. Stir in the prawns and squid and cook for a further 3–4 minutes until the prawns turn pink and the squid is cooked through.

Sprinkle with parsley, season and serve with crusty gluten-free bread, if liked.

For seafood salad, heat 2 tablespoons olive oil in a wok or frying pan, add 2 chopped garlic cloves and cook for 1 minute, then stir in 16 large raw peeled prawns and 300 g (10 oz) cleaned and sliced squid and stir-fry for 3–4 minutes until the prawns turn pink and the squid is cooked through. Toss with the leaves of 2 torn romaine lettuces and 50 g (2 oz) mangetout. Serve with a squeeze of lime juice. **Calories per serving 165**

falafel burgers with avocado salsa

Calories per serving **299**
Serves **4**
Preparation time **15 minutes,
    plus chilling**
Cooking time **6–8 minutes**

400 g (13 oz) can **chickpeas**,
    rinsed and drained
2 **spring onions**, chopped
2 **garlic cloves**, chopped
handful of **parsley**
1 teaspoon **ground cumin**
1 teaspoon **ground coriander**
½ teaspoon **harissa paste**
grated rind and juice of ½ **lime**
2 tablespoons **rice flour**
2 tablespoons **sunflower oil**
salt and **pepper**
watercress, to serve

Salsa
4 ripe **tomatoes**, diced
1 **avocado**, peeled, stoned
    and diced
½ small **red onion**, diced
1 tablespoon **extra virgin
    olive oil**
grated rind and juice of ½ **lime**

Place the chickpeas, spring onions, garlic, parsley,
spices, harissa, lime rind and juice and flour in a blender
or food processor. Season with salt and pepper and
blitz until fairly smooth. Using your hands, shape the
mixture into 4 patties, then chill for 20 minutes.

Meanwhile, make the salsa. Mix together all the
ingredients and set aside.

Heat the sunflower oil in a frying pan and cook the
burgers for 3–4 minutes on each side until lightly
golden and heated through.

Serve with watercress and the salsa.

For avocado with hummus, place a rinsed and
drained 400 g (13 oz) can chickpeas and 2 peeled
garlic cloves in a food processor and pulse until broken
down. Add 2 tablespoons tahini and the juice of 1 lime
and process until smooth. With the motor still running,
slowly pour in 100ml (3½ fl oz) olive oil until you have
the consistency you like (a little water can be added
to loosen, if needed). Peel and stone 2 avocados, then
slice thickly and divide between 4 plates. Serve with the
hummus and a squeeze of lemon juice, sprinkled with
pepper. **Calories per serving 468**

roasted cod with ratatouille

Calories per serving **269**
Serves **4**
Preparation time **10 minutes**
Cooking time **26–28 minutes**

400 g (13 oz) **courgettes**,
  sliced
2 **red peppers**, cored,
  deseeded and chopped
2 **red onions**, cut into wedges
1 **aubergine**, chopped
4 **garlic cloves**, sliced
2 tablespoons **olive oil**
300 g (10 oz) **cherry
  tomatoes**
small handful of **basil leaves**,
  torn
4 **cod loins**, about 150 g
  (5 oz) each
salt and **pepper**

Place the vegetables in a roasting tin and toss together with the garlic, oil and salt and pepper. Place in a preheated oven, 220°C (425°F), Gas Mark 7, for 16 minutes.

Add the tomatoes and basil to the vegetables and toss together. Nestle the cod loins among the vegetables, then return to the oven for a further 10–12 minutes, or until the fish is cooked through.

For baked cod, tomatoes & leeks, place 4 x 150 g (5 oz) cod loins in a foil-lined ovenproof dish. Drizzle over 2 tablespoons olive oil and the juice of 1 lemon, then add 2 trimmed, cleaned and sliced leeks, 100 g (3½ oz) halved cherry tomatoes and salt and pepper. Toss together gently, then seal the foil to form a parcel. Place in a preheated oven, 200°C (400°F), Gas Mark 6, for 18–19 minutes, or until the fish is cooked through. Meanwhile, cook 475 g (15 oz) peeled and chopped potatoes in a saucepan of boiling water for 12–15 minutes until tender. Drain, then mash with 1 tablespoon natural yogurt, ½ tablespoon olive oil and 4 sliced spring onions. Serve the cod with the mashed potatoes. **Calories per serving 333**

quinoa & lamb stuffed peppers

Calories per serving **274**
Serves **4**
Preparation time **10 minutes**
Cooking time **35 minutes**

4 **red peppers**, halved, cored
   and deseeded
200 g (7 oz) **minced lamb**
1 **garlic clove**, crushed
2 teaspoons **ground cumin**
1 teaspoon **paprika**
50 g (2 oz) **quinoa**
250 ml (8 fl oz) **gluten-free
   vegetable stock**
1 tablespoon chopped **mint**
1 tablespoon chopped **parsley**
steamed **green beans** and
   courgettes, to serve

Place the pepper halves, cut side up, in a roasting tin
and roast in a preheated oven, 200°C (400°F), Gas
Mark 6, for 20 minutes until starting to soften.

Meanwhile, heat a nonstick frying pan, add the minced
lamb and cook until it starts to brown. Stir in the garlic
and spices and cook for 1 minute. Add the quinoa and
stock, cover and simmer for 10–12 minutes until the
quinoa is soft. Stir in the herbs.

Remove the roasted peppers from the oven and
spoon in the lamb mixture, then return to the oven for
a further 15 minutes. Serve with steamed green beans
and courgettes.

For lamb chops with peperonata, heat 1 tablespoon
olive oil in a pan, add 1 large sliced onion and cook for
2–3 minutes. Add 2 cored, deseeded and sliced red
peppers, 2 cored, deseeded and sliced yellow peppers,
2 sliced garlic cloves and ½ teaspoon dried oregano
and cook for 8–10 minutes, stirring frequently, until
softened. Add 4 chopped plum tomatoes and cook for
a further 1–2 minutes. Stir in a few chopped basil leaves
and season well. Meanwhile, grill 8 lamb cutlets until
cooked to your liking. Serve with the peperonata and a
squeeze of lemon juice. **Calories per serving 407**

oven-baked halibut

Calories per serving **227**
Serves **4**
Preparation time **15 minutes**
Cooking time **15 minutes**

4 **halibut fillets**, about 150 g
    (5 oz) each
4 **tomatoes**, chopped
4 **spring onions**, sliced
1 **red chilli**, deseeded and
    sliced
2 **garlic cloves**, sliced
2 **carrots**, peeled and cut into
    julienne strips
juice of 2 **limes**
2 tablespoons **gluten-free soy
    sauce**
few **coriander sprigs**
salt and **pepper**
steamed **green beans**, to
    serve

Place each halibut fillet on a large piece of nonstick
baking paper, then top each with a quarter of the
tomatoes and spring onions. Divide the remaining
ingredients between the fish and season with salt
and pepper.

Wrap up and seal the paper to form parcels, then
transfer to a baking sheet. Bake in a preheated oven,
220°C (425°F), Gas Mark 7, for 15 minutes, or until
the fish is cooked through. Serve with steamed
green beans.

For Thai-style halibut, heat ½ tablespoon olive oil
in a frying pan, add 6 chopped spring onions and
fry for 1 minute, then stir in 2 tablespoons red Thai
curry paste and cook for 1 minute. Stir in 200 ml
(7 fl oz) gluten-free fish stock and a 400 ml (14 fl oz)
can coconut milk. Bring to the boil, then reduce the
heat and simmer for 5 minutes. Add 4 x 150 g (5 oz)
halibut fillets, cover and cook for 6–8 minutes until
the fish is cooked through. Divide 150 g (5 oz) wilted
spinach between 4 bowls, then spoon in the halibut and
pour over the liquid. Serve sprinkled with 2 tablespoons
toasted sesame seeds. **Calories per serving 427**

thai sesame chicken patties

Calories per serving **286**
Serves **4**
Preparation time **15 minutes,
plus chilling**
Cooking time **10 minutes**

3 tablespoons **sesame seeds**
4 **spring onions**
15 g (½ oz) **coriander**, plus
extra to garnish
500 g (1 lb) **minced chicken**
1 tablespoon **gluten-free light
soy sauce**
3.5 cm (1½ inch) piece of
fresh root ginger, peeled
and finely grated
1 **egg white**
1 tablespoon **sesame oil**
1 tablespoon **sunflower oil**
spring onion curls, to garnish
(optional)
8 tablespoons **gluten-free
Thai sweet chilli dipping
sauce**, to serve

Heat a nonstick frying pan over a medium-low heat
and dry-fry the sesame seeds for 2 minutes, stirring
frequently, until golden brown and toasted. Set aside.

Place the spring onions and coriander in a food
processor and whizz until finely chopped. Alternatively,
chop with a knife. Transfer to a bowl and mix with the
chicken, toasted sesame seeds, soy sauce, ginger and
egg white.

Divide the mixture into 20 mounds on a chopping
board, then, using wet hands, shape into slightly
flattened rounds. Chill for 1 hour (or longer if you
have time).

Heat the sesame and sunflower oils in a large frying
pan, add the patties and fry for 10 minutes, turning
once or twice, until golden and cooked through to the
centre. Arrange on a serving plate and garnish with
extra coriander leaves and spring onion curls, if liked.
Serve with the chilli dipping sauce.

For baby leaf stir-fry with chilli, to serve as an
accompaniment, heat 2 teaspoons sesame oil in the
frying pan, add a 250 g (8 oz) pack ready-prepared
baby leaf and baby vegetable stir-fry ingredients and
stir-fry for 2–3 minutes until the vegetables are hot.
Mix in 2 tablespoons gluten-free light soy sauce and
1 tablespoon gluten-free Thai sweet chilli dipping
sauce. **Calories per serving 54**

seared steak with creamy beans

Calories per serving **270**
Serves **4**
Preparation time **5 minutes**
Cooking time **20–25 minutes**

1 tablespoon **olive oil**
2 large **leeks**, trimmed,
   cleaned and finely sliced
2 **garlic cloves**, finely chopped
400 g (13 oz) can **butter
   beans**, rinsed and drained
4 **fillet steaks**, about 150 g
   (5 oz) each
small bunch of **parsley**,
   chopped
1 tablespoon **natural yogurt**
2 tablespoons **extra virgin
   olive oil**
salt and **pepper**

Heat the oil in a frying pan, add the leeks and garlic
and sauté over a low heat for 12–15 minutes until soft.
Add the beans and enough water just to cover, then
simmer for 8–10 minutes until the beans are very soft.

Meanwhile, heat a griddle pan until very hot and cook
the steaks to your liking. Leave to rest.

Stir the parsley, yogurt and olive oil into the beans and
season with salt and pepper.

Slice the steaks into large chunks and serve on a bed
of creamy beans.

For spicy beans on toast, heat 1 tablespoon olive
oil in a frying pan, add 1 chopped leek and 1 cored,
deseeded and chopped red pepper and sauté for
5 minutes until softened. Stir in 2 rinsed and drained
400 g (13 oz) cans butter beans, 2 tablespoons
gluten-free tomato ketchup, ½ tablespoon gluten-free
Worcestershire sauce and 3 tablespoons water. Bring
to a simmer and cook for 10–12 minutes. Season to
taste, then add 2 tablespoons chopped parsley and
2 tablespoons flaked almonds. Toast 4 slices of gluten-
free bread and spoon over the beans to serve. **Calories
per serving 310**

chicken with peppers

Calories per serving **241**
Serves **4**
Preparation time **10 minutes**
Cooking time **1 hour**

6 **tomatoes**, quartered
2 **red onions**, cut into thick
   wedges
1 **red pepper**, cored,
   deseeded and chopped
1 **yellow pepper**, cored,
   deseeded and chopped
4 **garlic cloves**, crushed
small bunch of **thyme**, leaves
   only
1 teaspoon **smoked paprika**
2 tablespoons **olive oil**
1 tablespoon **balsamic
   vinegar**
4 **boneless, skinless chicken
   thighs**, about 300 g (10 oz)
   in total
crisp green salad, to serve

Place all the ingredients except the chicken in a roasting tin and toss together, then top with the chicken.

Roast in a preheated oven, 180°C (350°F), Gas Mark 4, for 1 hour, turning and basting occasionally, until the chicken is golden and cooked through. Serve with a crisp green salad.

For chicken & red pepper open sandwiches,
spread 4 slices of gluten-free bread with 1 teaspoon pesto each. Top each one with 1 sliced, roasted red pepper, ½ sliced ready-cooked chicken breast and a few rocket leaves. Sprinkle with pepper and a drizzle of balsamic glaze, then serve immediately. **Calories per serving 266**

provençal fish stew

Calories per serving **234**
Serves **4**
Preparation time **15 minutes**
Cooking time **15–18 minutes**

1 tablespoon **olive oil**
3 **shallots**, thinly sliced
3 **garlic cloves**, chopped
400 g (13 oz) can **chopped tomatoes**
1 tablespoon **tomato purée**
1 **thyme sprig**
300 ml (½ pint) **gluten-free fish stock**
300 g (10 oz) **live mussels**, scrubbed and debearded (discard any that don't shut when tapped)
500 g (1 lb) **skinless cod** or **haddock fillet**, cut into pieces
200 g (7 oz) **squid**, cleaned and sliced into rings
salt and **pepper**
2 tablespoons chopped **parsley**, to garnish

Heat the oil in a large pan, add the shallots and garlic and fry for 3–4 minutes until softened. Add the tomatoes, tomato purée and thyme and cook for a further 4–5 minutes.

Pour in the stock and bring to the boil, then add the mussels, fish and squid, cover the pan and cook for 5–6 minutes until the mussels have opened and the fish is cooked through. Discard any mussels that remain closed.

Season with salt and pepper, ladle into 4 bowls and serve sprinkled with parsley.

For hot & sour fish soup, place 850 ml (1½ pints) hot gluten-free fish stock, 1 teaspoon coriander seeds and 2.5 cm (1 inch) piece of fresh root ginger, peeled and sliced, in a saucepan and simmer for 5 minutes. Add 1 tablespoon gluten-free fish sauce, 2 thinly sliced red chillies and 3 thinly sliced garlic cloves and simmer for a further 2 minutes, then add 300 g (10 oz) raw peeled king prawns and 200 g (7 oz) skinless cod or haddock fillet, cut into pieces, and cook gently for 5–6 minutes until the prawns turn pink and the fish is cooked through. Add 2 sliced spring onions and the juice of 1 lime. Season to taste and serve sprinkled with 2 tablespoons chopped coriander. **Calories per serving 128**

aubergine bake

Calories per serving **297 (not including salad and bread)**
Serves **4**
Preparation time **10 minutes**
Cooking time **40–45 minutes**

2 **large aubergines**, sliced
2 tablespoons **olive oil**
150 g (5 oz) **mozzarella cheese**, roughly chopped
4 tablespoons grated **Parmesan cheese**
salt and **pepper**

Tomato sauce
1 tablespoon **olive oil**
1 **garlic clove**, crushed
1 small **onion**, finely chopped
400 g (13 oz) can **plum tomatoes**
handful of **basil**, torn

Make the tomato sauce. Heat the oil in a saucepan, add the garlic and onion and fry for 3–4 minutes until softened. Add the tomatoes and basil, bring to the boil, then reduce the heat and simmer for 15 minutes.

Brush the aubergines with the oil on each side while the sauce is simmering. Heat a griddle pan until hot and cook the aubergine slices for 1–2 minutes on each side until tender and browned.

Spoon a little of the tomato sauce into an ovenproof dish, layer over half the aubergines, scatter over half the mozzarella and Parmesan and season well. Repeat the layering with the remaining ingredients, finishing with a scattering of the cheeses.

Place in a preheated oven, 200°C (400°F), Gas Mark 6, for 20–25 minutes until golden and bubbling. Serve with salad and gluten-free crusty bread, if liked.

For aubergine, chilli & chicken bake, make the tomato sauce as above, adding 1 deseeded and finely sliced red chilli with the garlic and onion. Cook the aubergine and layer the bake as above, interspersing 300 g (10 oz) torn cooked chicken between the aubergine layers. Cook in the oven as above. **Calories per serving 382**

thai steamed fish

Calories per serving **210**
(not including rice, pak choi
and mange tout)
Serves **4**
Preparation time **10 minutes**
Cooking time **10 minutes**

4 **trout fillets**, about 150 g
(5 oz) each
4 **pak choi**, quartered
lengthways
5 cm (2 inch) piece of **fresh**
root ginger, peeled and
sliced
2 **garlic cloves**, chopped
1 **red chilli**, deseeded and
sliced
grated rind and juice of 2
limes
3 tablespoons **gluten-free soy**
sauce

Place the trout fillets and pak choi on 2 large pieces
of foil and sprinkle with the ginger, garlic, chilli, lime
rind and juice. Pour over the soy sauce, then loosely
seal the foil to form parcels.

Transfer the parcels to a steamer and cook for
10 minutes, or until the fish is cooked through.
Serve with lime halves, jasmine rice and steamed pak
choi and mange tout, if liked.

For Thai fish soup, mix together 1 litre (1¾ pints)
gluten-free fish stock, 1½ tablespoons red Thai curry
paste, 4 kaffir lime leaves and 1 tablespoon gluten-free
fish sauce in a saucepan. Bring to a simmer and cook
for 5 minutes, then add 300 g (10 oz) skinless white
fish fillets, such as cod or haddock, and cook for
2 minutes. Stir in 150 g (5 oz) raw peeled king prawns,
3 pak choi, quartered, and a handful of coriander leaves
and simmer for 2–3 minutes until the prawns turn pink
and the fish is just cooked through. Serve immediately.
Calories per serving 148

mediterranean squid

Calories per serving **257**
Serves **4**
Preparation time **10 minutes**
Cooking time **25 minutes**

1 tablespoon **olive oil**
1 **red onion**, diced
1 **garlic clove**, sliced
75 g (3 oz) **pitted black olives**
1 **red chilli**, deseeded and
  finely sliced
pinch of **paprika**
400 g (13 oz) can **chopped
  tomatoes**
400 g (13 oz) can **butter
  beans**, rinsed and drained
600 g (1¼ lb) **squid**, cleaned
  and sliced into rings
grated rind of 1 **lemon**
small handful of **parsley**,
  chopped
salt and **pepper**
lemon wedges, to serve

Heat the oil in a large pan, add the onion and garlic and
fry for 3–4 minutes until softened. Add the olives, chilli
and paprika and cook for a further 1 minute. Stir in the
tomatoes and simmer for 12 minutes.

Add the butter beans and season well. Bring to the boil,
then add the squid, cover and simmer for 5–6 minutes
until the squid is cooked through and tender.

Sprinkle with the lemon rind and chopped parsley
and serve with lemon wedges.

For salt & pepper squid, mix together 85 g (3 oz)
gram flour, 85 g (3 oz) rice flour, 2 tablespoons crushed
Sichuan peppercorns, 2 teaspoons cracked black
pepper and 1 teaspoon sea salt in a bowl. Heat about
7 cm (3 inches) vegetable oil in a deep pan or wok to
180–190°C (350–375°F), or until a cube of gluten-
free bread browns in 30 seconds. Cut 400 g (13 oz)
cleaned squid into rings, then coat in the seasoned
flour and deep-fry in batches for about 2–3 minutes
until golden. Remove with a slotted spoon and drain
on kitchen paper, sprinkling with a little more salt.
Serve sprinkled with a few chopped spring onions
and a dipping sauce. **Calories per serving 232
(not including dipping sauce)**

chicken with mango salsa

Calories per serving **265**
Serves **4**
Preparation time **10 minutes**
Cooking time **6–8 minutes**

1 large **mango**, peeled, stoned
and diced
1 small **red onion**, diced
1 **red chilli**, deseeded and
finely diced
large bunch of **parsley**,
chopped
2 tablespoons **olive oil**
juice of ½ **lime**
4 **boneless, skinless chicken
breasts**, about 150 g (5 oz)
each
2 **garlic cloves**, halved
pepper

Mix together the mango, red onion, chilli, parsley,
1 tablespoon of the oil and the lime juice in a bowl.
Set aside.

Place the chicken breasts between 2 sheets of
nonstick baking paper or clingfilm and flatten with
a rolling pin or mallet. Rub with the cut garlic, sprinkle
with pepper and drizzle with the remaining oil.

Heat a large griddle pan over a medium-high heat and
cook the chicken for 3–4 minutes on each side until
cooked through. Serve with the salsa.

For chicken & mango toasts, spread 4 slices of
gluten-free wholemeal bread with 1 tablespoon
gluten-free mango chutney each, then top each one
with 3–4 spinach leaves, a few coriander leaves and
50 g (2 oz) sliced ready-cooked chicken. Sprinkle over
75 g (3 oz) grated Cheddar cheese and cook under
a preheated grill for 3–4 minutes until bubbling and
golden. **Calories per serving 294**

mini smoked trout quiches

Calories per serving **295**
Serves **4**
Preparation time **10 minutes**
Cooking time **12–15 minutes**

½ tablespoon **rapeseed oil**
400 g (13 oz) **baby spinach leaves**
6 large **eggs**
100 ml (3½ fl oz) **semi-skimmed milk**
3 tablespoons grated **Parmesan cheese**
2 tablespoons finely chopped **chives**
150 g (5 oz) **hot-smoked trout fillets**, flaked
4 **cherry tomatoes**, halved
salt and **pepper**

Line 8 holes of a muffin tin with 15 cm (6 inch) squares of greaseproof paper.

Heat the oil in a frying pan, add the spinach and cook briefly until wilted. Remove from the heat.

Beat together the eggs, milk and cheese in a jug and season to taste, then stir in the chives and trout.

Divide the spinach between the muffin cases, then pour in the egg mixture. Top each one with half a cherry tomato.

Bake in a preheated oven, 180°C (350°F), Gas Mark 4, for 12–15 minutes until just set.

For smoked trout baked eggs, brush 4 ramekins with melted butter, then add 50 g (2 oz) flaked hot-smoked trout fillet to each dish. Carefully break 2 eggs into each ramekin, top with 2 tablespoons grated Cheddar cheese and season. Place the ramekins in a roasting tin with enough boiling water to come three-quarters of the way up the sides of the dishes. Bake in a preheated oven, 200°C (400°F), Gas Mark 6, for 8–9 minutes until the cheese has melted and the egg is cooked but still soft. **Calories per serving 244**

vegetable & feta fritters

Calories per serving **207**
Serves **4**
Preparation time **10 minutes**
Cooking time **6–12 minutes**

1 **large courgette**, grated
grated rind of 1 **lemon**
2 **spring onions**, sliced
2 tablespoons chopped
   parsley
2 tablespoons chopped **mint**
100 g (3½ oz) **feta cheese**,
   crumbled
2 tablespoons **rice flour**
1 **egg yolk**
2 **ready-cooked fresh**
   beetroots, peeled and
   grated
2 tablespoons **olive oil**
salt and **pepper**
basil leaves, to garnish
mixed leaf salad, to serve

Mix together the courgette, lemon rind, spring onions, herbs, feta, rice flour and egg yolk in a large bowl and season well. Gently stir in the beetroot until the mixture is just speckled with red.

Heat a little of the oil in a frying pan, add tablespoons of the mixture to the pan and fry the fritters for 1–2 minutes on each side until golden. Transfer to a serving plate and keep warm. Repeat with the remaining mixture, adding the remaining oil to the pan as necessary.

Garnish the fritters with basil leaves and serve with a mixed leaf salad.

For cucumber & yogurt dip, to serve as an accompaniment, mix together 200 ml (7 fl oz) fat-free Greek yogurt, 1 crushed garlic clove, 1 teaspoon toasted cumin seeds, ¼ grated cucumber, squeezed of excess liquid, and a pinch of paprika in a serving dish. Season well. **Calories per serving 33**

cheese & herb scones

Calories per scone **222 (not including butter to serve)**
Makes **12**
Preparation time **15 minutes**
Cooking time **15 minutes**

350 g (11½ oz) **gluten-free self-raising flour**, plus extra for dusting
1 teaspoon **gluten-free baking powder**
1 teaspoon **mustard powder**
pinch of **cayenne pepper**
60 g (2¼ oz) **unsalted butter**, diced
200 g (7 oz) **Cheddar cheese**, grated
1 tablespoon chopped **chives**, or herb of your choice
2 large **eggs**
5–6 tablespoons **buttermilk**

Sift the flour, baking powder, mustard powder and cayenne into a large bowl. Add the butter and rub in with the fingertips until the mixture resembles breadcrumbs. Mix in 175g (6 oz) of the grated cheese and the herbs.

Beat the eggs with the buttermilk in a jug, then mix into the flour to form a soft dough – do not overwork the dough. Turn out on to a lightly floured work surface and roll out to a thickness of 2.5 cm (1 inch). Stamp out 12 scones using a 4–5 cm (2 inch) cutter and place on a baking sheet.

Sprinkle the remaining cheese over the scones and bake in a preheated oven, 220°C (425°F), Gas Mark 7, for 15 minutes until risen and golden. Serve the scones warm, with butter, if liked.

For cheese & herb muffins, mix together 100 g (3½ oz) polenta, 125 g (4 oz) almond flour, 100 g (3½ oz) tapioca flour, 3 teaspoons gluten-free baking powder, ¼ teaspoon paprika, 100 g (3½ oz) grated Cheddar cheese and 2 tablespoons chopped chives. Mix together 125 ml (4 fl oz) sunflower oil, 2 eggs and 225 ml (7½ fl oz) milk, then mix the liquid into dry ingredients to make a batter. Line a 12-hole muffin tin with paper muffin cases and spoon in the mixture. Sprinkle each one with 5 g (¼ oz) grated Cheddar and bake in a preheated oven, 190°C (375°F), Gas Mark 5, for 17–18 minutes until golden. **Calories per muffin 351**

cottage cheese & chive muffins

Calories per muffin **231**
Makes **12**
Preparation time **10 minutes**
Cooking time **30–35 minutes**

225 g (7½ oz) **cottage cheese**
100 g (3½ oz) **gluten-free plain flour**
150 g (5 oz) **ground almonds**
100 g (3½ oz) **sun-dried tomatoes**, drained and chopped
2 teaspoons chopped **chives**
1 teaspoon **gluten-free baking powder**
75 g (3 oz) **Parmesan cheese**, grated
3 tablespoons **sunflower oil**
4 large **eggs**, beaten
1 tablespoon **cold water**
salt and **pepper**

Line a 12-hole muffin tin with paper muffin cases.

Place the cottage cheese, flour, ground almonds, tomatoes, chives, baking powder and half of the cheese in a bowl. Add the oil, eggs and measurement water, season lightly and gently mix together. Do not overmix.

Spoon the batter into the muffin cases and sprinkle with the remaining cheese. Bake in a preheated oven, 200°C (400°F), Gas Mark 6, for 30–35 minutes until risen and golden. Serve warm.

For cottage cheese & chive snacks, mix together ½ tablespoon cottage cheese, 2 tablespoons drained and chopped sun-dried tomatoes and 1 tablespoon chopped chives in a bowl. Divide the mixture between 12 gluten-free oatcakes, then sprinkle each one with ½ teaspoon grated Parmesan cheese and serve immediately. **Calories per snack 73**

lemon & raspberry cupcakes

Calories per cupcake **290**
Makes **12**
Preparation time **10 minutes**
Cooking time **12–15 minutes**

150 g (5 oz) **butter**, softened
150 g (5 oz) **caster sugar**
75 g (3 oz) **rice flour**
75 g (3 oz) **cornflour**
1 tablespoon **gluten-free
    baking powder**
grated rind and juice of 1
    lemon
3 **eggs**, beaten
125 g (4 oz) **raspberries**
1 tablespoon **gluten-free
    lemon curd**

Line a large 12-hole muffin tin with large paper muffin cases.

Whisk together all the ingredients except the raspberries and lemon curd in a large bowl. Fold in the raspberries.

Spoon half the sponge mixture into the muffin cases, dot over a little of the lemon curd, then add the remaining sponge mixture.

Bake in a preheated oven, 200°C (400°F), Gas Mark 6, for 12–15 minutes until golden and firm to the touch. Remove from the oven, transfer to a wire rack and leave to cool.

For citrusy muffins, make the sponge mixture as above, adding the grated rind of 1 orange. Omit the raspberries and lemon curd and cook as above. Mix 150 g (5 oz) icing sugar and 1–2 teaspoons lemon juice in a bowl to make a fairly thick icing and drizzle over the cooled muffins. Decorate with gluten-free lemon and orange jelly sweets, if liked. **Calories per muffin 265 (not including sweets)**

apricot & treacle flapjacks

Calories per square **226**
Makes **12**
Preparation time **5 minutes**
Cooking time **25 minutes**

100 g (3½ oz) **coconut oil**,
   plus extra for greasing
75 g (3 oz) **black treacle**
20 g (¾ oz) **dark muscovado**
   sugar
40 g (1½ oz) **golden syrup**
235 g (8 oz) **gluten-free**
   rolled oats
50 g (2 oz) **ready-to-eat dried**
   apricots, chopped
50 g (2 oz) **pumpkin seeds**
grated rind of **1 orange**

Grease an 18 cm (7 inch) square baking tin with coconut oil.

Melt together the coconut oil, treacle, sugar and syrup in a large saucepan, stirring until the sugar has dissolved. Add the remaining ingredients and mix well. Spoon the mixture into the prepared tin and level the top.

Bake in a preheated oven, 180°C (350°F), Gas Mark 4, for 18–20 minutes until golden. Leave to cool in the tin for 2 minutes before cutting into squares, then leave to cool completely in the tin. Store in an airtight container and eat within 5–6 days.

For festive flapjacks, melt together the coconut oil and sugar with 25 g (1 oz) black treacle and 90 g (3¼ oz) golden syrup, stirring until the sugar has dissolved. Add 230 g (7½ oz) gluten-free rolled oats, 1 tablespoon sultanas, 1 tablespoon mixed peel and 1 teaspoon ground cinnamon and mix well. Spoon into a greased 18 cm (7 inch) square baking tin and level the top. Bake and cut into squares as above.
Calories per square 198

creamy mango smoothie

Calories per serving **282**
Serves **4**
Preparation time **10 minutes**

4 **ripe mangoes**, peeled and
   stoned
4 tablespoons **natural yogurt**
1 **banana**, chopped
1 litre (1¾ pints)
   unsweetened soya milk
2 teaspoons **clear honey**
   (optional)
ice cubes, to serve

Place all the ingredients except the honey and ice in a blender or food processor and blend until smooth. Taste for sweetness and add the honey, if required, then blend again.

Pour into 4 tall glasses and serve with ice cubes.

For marinated mango salad, toss together 4 peeled, stoned and chopped mangoes, 2 segmented oranges, 150 g (5 oz) blueberries and 1 tablespoon shredded mint leaves in a non-metallic bowl. Mix together 1 tablespoon clear honey, the grated rind and juice of 2 limes and ¼ teaspoon ground cinnamon in a separate bowl. Pour the marinade over the mango salad and leave to marinate at room temperature for 25 minutes. Divide between 4 bowls and serve each with 1 tablespoon half-fat crème fraîche. **Calories per serving 287**

griddled bananas with blueberries

Calories per serving **258**
Serves **4**
Preparation time **5 minutes**
Cooking time **8–10 minutes**

4 **bananas**, unpeeled
8 tablespoons **fat-free Greek yogurt**
4 tablespoons **gluten-free oatmeal** or **fine porridge oats**
125 g (4 oz) **blueberries**
4 teaspoons **clear honey**, to serve

Heat a ridged griddle pan over a medium-high heat, add the bananas and griddle for 8–10 minutes, or until the skins are beginning to blacken, turning occasionally.

Transfer the bananas to 4 serving dishes and, using a sharp knife, cut open lengthways. Spoon over the yogurt and sprinkle with the oatmeal or oats and blueberries. Serve immediately, drizzled with the honey.

For oatmeal, ginger & sultana yogurt, mix

½ teaspoon ground ginger with the yogurt in a bowl. Sprinkle with 2–4 tablespoons soft dark brown sugar, according to taste, the oatmeal and 4 level tablespoons sultanas. Leave to stand for 5 minutes before serving. **Calories per serving 219**

spiced plum hazelnut meringue

Calories per serving **274**
Serves **8**
Preparation time **15 minutes, plus cooling**
Cooking time **2 hours**

5 **egg whites**
250 g (8 oz) **caster sugar**
100 g (3½ oz) **roasted chopped hazelnuts**
8 **plums**, halved and stoned
½ teaspoon **mixed spice**
2 tablespoons **dark muscovado sugar**
juice of **1 orange**
250 ml (8 fl oz) **fat-free Greek yogurt**

Line a baking sheet with nonstick baking paper.

Whisk the egg whites in a large clean bowl until stiff peaks form, then add ½ tablespoon of the caster sugar at a time, whisking well between each addition, until the mixture is very thick and glossy. Fold in the hazelnuts.

Spoon the meringue on to the prepared baking sheet in large dollops that join up to make a circle. Make a shallow dip in the centre with the back of a spoon.

Bake in a preheated oven, 140°C (275°F), Gas Mark 1, for 2 hours until pale golden and crisp. Turn off the oven and leave the meringue inside to cool completely.

Place the plums in a heatproof dish, cut side up, and sprinkle with the mixed spice, brown sugar and orange juice. Cook under a preheated hot grill until bubbling and golden. Leave to cool slightly.

Spoon the yogurt into the centre of the meringue and spoon over the plums to serve.

For plum Eton mess, halve, stone and cut the plums into quarters, then place in a roasting tin and sprinkle with the mixed spice, dark muscovado sugar and orange juice. Roast in a preheated oven, 180°C (350°F), Gas Mark 4 for 15–20 minutes until tender. Leave to cool, then stir in 600 g (1¼ lb) fat-free Greek yogurt and 4 crushed ready-made meringue nests. Divide between 8 bowls and serve sprinkled with 1 tablespoon chopped hazelnuts. **Calories per serving 109**

spiced baked pears

Calories per serving **218**
Serves **4**
Preparation time **10 minutes**
Cooking time **35–40 minutes**

4 **pears**, peeled, halved and
    cored
125 ml (4 fl oz) **apple juice**
75 ml (3 fl oz) **maple syrup**
1 **vanilla pod**, split in half
    lengthways
grated rind of 1 **lemon**
grated rind of 1 **orange**
5 **cardamom pods**, bruised
3 **star anise**
3 **cloves**
2 tablespoons **toasted flaked
    almonds**, to decorate
2 tablespoons **fat-free Greek
    yogurt**, to serve

Place the pears, cut side up, in an ovenproof dish. Pour over the apple juice and maple syrup, then scrape over the seeds from the vanilla pod. Sprinkle with the grated citrus rind and spices. Cover with foil.

Bake in a preheated oven, 200°C (400°F), Gas Mark 6, for 20 minutes, then turn the pears over and cook, covered, for a further 15–20 minutes until tender.

Spoon the pears into 4 serving bowls, pour over the juices and sprinkle with the almonds. Serve with dollops of the yogurt.

For cinnamon porridge with grated pears, place 125 g (4 oz) gluten-free porridge oats and ½ teaspoon ground cinnamon in a pan with 600 ml (1 pint) semi-skimmed milk and cook over a medium heat for 5–6 minutes, stirring constantly, until thick and creamy. Pour into 4 bowls and grate over 4 pears. Serve with a squeeze of lemon juice and sprinkling of ground cinnamon. **Calories per serving 279**

yogurt & berry smoothie

Calories per serving **232**

Serves **4**

Preparation time **5 minutes**

300 ml (½ pint) **natural yogurt**

500 g (1 lb) **fresh** or **frozen mixed summer berries**, defrosted if frozen, plus extra to decorate

4 tablespoons **millet flakes**

3 tablespoons **clear honey**

300 ml (½ pint) **cranberry juice**

Place all the ingredients in a food processor or a blender and blitz until smooth.

Pour into 4 glasses, decorate with a few extra whole berries and serve immediately.

For frozen raspberry yogurt slice, blitz 500 g (1 lb) raspberries, 200 g (7 oz) icing sugar, the juice of 1 lemon and 600 ml (1 pint) fat-free Greek yogurt in a food processor or blender. Pour the mixture into a 900 g (2 lb) loaf tin that has been lined with clingfilm, then freeze until solid. Serve sliced with 320 g (11 oz) mixed berries. **Calories per serving 374**

lemon, pistachio & fruit squares

Calories per square **255**
Makes **15**
Preparation time **10 minutes,**
  plus chilling
Cooking time **20 minutes**

butter, for greasing
grated rind of **1 lemon**
75 g (3 oz) **ready-to-eat dried**
  dates, chopped
75 g (3 oz) **unsalted**
  pistachio nuts, chopped
75 g (3 oz) **flaked almonds**,
  chopped
125 g (4 oz) **soft light brown**
  sugar
150 g (5 oz) **millet flakes**
40 g (1½ oz) **gluten-free**
  cornflakes, lightly crushed
400 g (13 oz) can **condensed**
  milk
25 g (1 oz) **mixed pumpkin**
  and sunflower seeds

Grease a 28 x 18 cm (11 x 7 inch) baking tin with butter.

Mix together all the ingredients in a large bowl until well combined and spoon the mixture into the prepared tin.

Place in a preheated oven, 180°C (350°F), Gas Mark 4, for 20 minutes. Leave to cool in the tin, then mark into 15 squares and chill until firm. Store in an airtight container and eat within 3–5 days.

For chocolate fruit & nut squares, place 75 g (3 oz) gluten-free white chocolate and 75 g (3 oz) gluten-free plain dark chocolate in separate heatproof bowls over saucepans of simmering water and leave until melted. Drizzle over the cooked and cooled squares and leave to set. **Calories per square 309**

recipes under 400 calories

avocado, pepper & olive salad

Calories per serving **342**
Serves **4**
Preparation time **10 minutes**
Cooking time **2 minutes**

1 tablespoon **sesame seeds**
2 **avocados**, peeled, stoned
    and chopped
juice of 1 **lime**
1 **red pepper**, cored,
    deseeded and chopped
1 **yellow pepper**, cored,
    deseeded and chopped
½ **cucumber**, finely chopped
2 **carrots**, peeled and
    chopped
2 **tomatoes**, chopped
4 **spring onions**, sliced
10 **pitted black olives**, halved
1 **romaine lettuce**, roughly
    torn
4 tablespoons **gluten-free
    French dressing**
1 tablespoon chopped **mint**

Heat a nonstick frying pan over a medium-low heat and dry-fry the sesame seeds for 2 minutes, stirring frequently, until golden brown and toasted. Set aside.

Meanwhile, place the avocados in a large bowl and toss with the lime juice to prevent discoloration. Gently toss together with the remaining ingredients except the sesame seeds.

Sprinkle the salad with the toasted sesame seeds and serve.

For peperonata with avocado & olives, heat 3 tablespoons olive oil in a frying pan, add 2 sliced garlic cloves and 3 sliced onions and cook for 1–2 minutes. Core, deseed and slice 2 red peppers and 2 yellow peppers, then add to the pan and cook for 10 minutes. Add 350 g (11½ oz) chopped ripe tomatoes and cook for a further 12–15 minutes until the peppers are soft. Stir in 1 peeled, stoned and chopped avocado, 12 halved pitted black olives and a small handful of basil leaves. Serve with gluten-free crusty bread, if liked. **Calories per serving 307 (not including bread)**

roasted butternut & cashew soup

Calories per serving **317**
Serves **4**
Preparation time **10 minutes**
Cooking time **25 minutes**

1 kg (2 lb) **butternut squash**,
  peeled, deseeded and
  chopped into 1 cm (½ inch)
  chunks
2 tablespoons **olive oil**
1 tablespoon chopped **sage**
2 tablespoons **pumpkin
  seeds**
1 **onion**, chopped
1 **garlic clove**, chopped
½ tablespoon **mild curry
  powder**
2 tablespoons **cashew nuts**
600 ml (1 pint) hot **gluten-free
  vegetable stock**
8 tablespoons **natural yogurt**
salt and **pepper**

Place the squash in a roasting tin and toss with 1 tablespoon of the oil and the sage. Place in a preheated oven, 220°C (425°F), Gas Mark 7, for 18–20 minutes until tender and golden.

Meanwhile, heat a nonstick frying pan over a medium-low heat and dry-fry the pumpkin seeds for 2–3 minutes, stirring frequently, until golden brown and toasted. Set aside.

Heat the remaining oil in a saucepan, add the onion and garlic and cook for 4–5 minutes until softened. Stir in the curry powder and cook for a further minute, stirring.

Add the roasted squash, cashews and stock and bring to the boil, then reduce the heat and simmer for 3–4 minutes. Stir in the yogurt. Using a hand-held blender, blend the soup until smooth. Season to taste.

Ladle the soup into 4 bowls and serve sprinkled with the toasted pumpkin seeds.

For butternut & sage colcannon, cook 750 g (1¾ lb) peeled, deseeded and chopped butternut squash and 300 g (10 oz) peeled and chopped potatoes in a saucepan of boiling water for 12–15 minutes until tender. Meanwhile, cook ½ shredded Savoy cabbage in a separate pan of boiling water for 4–5 minutes, then drain and keep warm. Meanwhile, poach 4 eggs (see page 32). Drain the squash and potatoes, then mash in the pan with 1 tablespoon natural yogurt, 1 tablespoon chopped sage and 25 g (1 oz) butter. Season well and stir in the cabbage. Serve topped with the poached eggs. **Calories per serving 300**

gingered cauliflower soup

Calories per serving **347**
Serves **6**
Preparation time **15 minutes**
Cooking time **25 minutes**

1 tablespoon **sunflower oil**
25 g (1 oz) **butter**
1 **onion**, roughly chopped
1 **cauliflower**, cut into florets,
  woody core discarded, about
  500 g (1 lb) when prepared
3.5 cm (1½ inch) piece of
  fresh root ginger, peeled
  and finely chopped
900 ml (1½ pints) **gluten-free**
  vegetable or **chicken stock**
300 ml (½ pint) **semi-**
  skimmed milk
150 ml (¼ pint) **double cream**
salt and **pepper**

Soy-glazed seeds
1 tablespoon **sunflower oil**
2 tablespoons **sesame seeds**
2 tablespoons **sunflower**
  seeds
2 tablespoons **pumpkin seeds**
1 tablespoon **gluten-free soy**
  sauce

Heat the oil and butter in a saucepan, add the onion and fry for 5 minutes until softened but not coloured. Stir in the cauliflower florets and ginger, then the stock. Season with salt and pepper and bring to the boil. Cover and simmer for 15 minutes until the cauliflower is just tender.

Meanwhile, make the glazed seeds. Heat the oil in a frying pan, add the seeds and cook for 2–3 minutes, stirring until lightly browned. Add the soy sauce, then quickly cover the pan with a lid until the seeds have stopped popping. Set aside.

Purée the cooked soup in batches in a blender or food processor, then pour back into the saucepan and stir in the milk and half the cream. Bring just to the boil, then taste and adjust the seasoning if needed.

Ladle the soup into 6 shallow bowls, drizzle over the remaining cream and sprinkle with some of the glazed seeds, serving the remaining seeds in a small bowl for further sprinkling.

For creamy cauliflower & cashew soup, heat the oil and butter as above, then add the chopped onion and 50 g (2 oz) cashew nuts and fry until the onions are softened and the nuts very lightly coloured. Mix in the cauliflower florets and stock as above, then season with salt, pepper and a little grated nutmeg. Simmer for 15 minutes. Meanwhile, fry 50 g (2 oz) cashew nuts in 15 g (½ oz) butter until pale golden, add 1 tablespoon honey and cook for 1–2 minutes until golden and caramelized. Purée the soup and finish with milk and cream as above, ladle into 6 bowls and garnish with the cashews. **Calories per serving 340**

spicy prawn tacos

Calories per serving **365**
Serves **4**
Preparation time **10 minutes,
plus marinating**
Cooking time **3 minutes**

1 tablespoon **olive oil**
juice of **1 lime**
2 **garlic cloves**, peeled and
crushed
½ **red chilli**, deseeded and
finely chopped
400 g (13 oz) **raw peeled
king prawns**
8 **gluten-free corn taco
shells**
1 **romaine lettuce**, shredded
200 g (7 oz) **ready-made
guacamole**
200 g (7 oz) **ready-made
tomato salsa**

Mix together the oil, lime juice, garlic and chilli in a non-metallic dish, then stir in the prawns. Leave to marinate for 20 minutes.

Heat the tacos according to the packet instructions.

Meanwhile, heat a nonstick frying pan, add the prawns and cook for 2–3 minutes until the prawns turn pink and are cooked through.

Stuff the tacos with shredded lettuce, then top with the prawns, guacamole and salsa and serve immediately.

For spicy prawn soup, pour 900 ml (1½ pints) gluten-free fish stock into a pan and add 2 chopped red chillies, 2 crushed garlic cloves, 1 crushed lemon grass stalk and a 2 cm (¾ inch) piece of fresh root ginger, peeled and sliced, and simmer for 15 minutes. Add 300 g (10 oz) raw peeled king prawns and 3 sliced spring onions and cook for 2–3 minutes until the prawns turn pink and are just cooked through, then stir in 2 chopped pak choi, a small bunch each of chopped mint and coriander and 50 g (2 oz) bean sprouts. Cook for a further 3–4 minutes, then squeeze in the juice of ½ lime and serve. **Calories per serving 101**

chicken balti with whole spices

Calories per serving **320 (not including rice)**
Serves **4**
Preparation time **20 minutes**
Cooking time **40 minutes**

1 **onion**, quartered
2.5 cm (1 inch) piece of **fresh root ginger**, peeled and sliced
3 **garlic cloves**
2 tablespoons **sunflower oil**
8 **boneless, skinless chicken thighs**, about 600 g (1¼ lb) in total, cubed
1 teaspoon **cumin seeds**, roughly crushed
1 **cinnamon stick**, halved
8 **cardamom pods**, roughly crushed
6 **cloves**
½ teaspoon **turmeric**
1 teaspoon **dried chilli flakes**
400 g (13 oz) can **chopped tomatoes**
600 ml (1 pint) **gluten-free chicken stock**
small bunch of **coriander**, torn
25 g (1 oz) **toasted flaked almonds,** to garnish

Place the onion, ginger and garlic in a food processor and whizz until finely chopped. Alternatively, chop with a knife.

Heat the oil in a medium saucepan, add the chicken and fry, stirring, for 5 minutes until lightly browned. Stir in the chopped onion mixture and fry for 2–3 minutes until softened.

Stir in the spices and chilli flakes and cook for 1 minute, then mix in the tomatoes and stock. Bring to the boil, then reduce the heat, cover and simmer for 30 minutes, stirring occasionally, until the chicken is cooked through.

Add the coriander and cook for 1 minute, then spoon into 4 bowls. Sprinkle with the almonds and serve with rice, if liked.

For chicken balti with mushrooms & spinach, omit the cumin seeds, cardamom, cloves, turmeric and chilli flakes and stir in 2 tablespoons medium-hot gluten-free balti curry paste instead. Mix in 125 g (4 oz) sliced cup mushrooms and cook as above. Stir in 150 g (5 oz) baby spinach leaves along with the coriander at the end and cook until the spinach has just wilted. **Calories per serving 324**

paneer & pepper tikka masala

Calories per serving **398**
(not including rice)
Serves **4**
Preparation time **10 minutes**
Cooking time **20–25 minutes**

½ tablespoon **sunflower oil**
225 g (7½ oz) **paneer
cheese**, cubed
2 **red peppers**, cored,
deseeded and chopped
2 **yellow peppers**, cored,
deseeded and chopped
2 **pak choi**, quartered
75 g (3 oz) **gluten-free tikka
masala curry paste**
150 ml (¼ pint) **reduced-fat
crème fraîche**
2 tablespoons chopped
coriander leaves

Heat the oil in a wok or frying pan, add the paneer
and cook for 4–5 minutes until golden. Remove with
a slotted spoon and drain on kitchen paper.

Add the peppers and pak choi to the pan and stir-fry
for 4–5 minutes until starting to soften. Stir in the
curry paste, add 4 tablespoons of water and cook for
a further 8–10 minutes.

Stir in the crème fraîche and simmer for 2 minutes,
then return the paneer to the pan with the coriander
and simmer for 2–3 minutes until heated through.
Serve with basmati rice, if liked.

For paneer-stuffed peppers, heat 1 tablespoon olive
oil in a frying pan, add ¼ teaspoon mustard seeds,
½ teaspoon turmeric, 1 teaspoon cumin seeds and
½ teaspoon paprika and cook until the mustard seeds
start to pop. Add 225 g (7½ oz) cubed paneer and
cook for 3–4 minutes until golden. Stir in 100 g (3½ oz)
frozen peas and 1 diced tomato and cook for 1 minute.
Cut 2 romano peppers in half, remove the seeds and
spoon the paneer mixture into each half. Place on a
baking sheet and roast in a preheated oven, 200°C
(400°F), Gas Mark 6, for 10–12 minutes until the
peppers have softened. **Calories per serving 270**

chicken salad wraps

Calories per serving **321**
Serves **4**
Preparation time **10 minutes**

4 **gluten-free ready-made
   tortillas**
4 tablespoons **gluten-free
   reduced-fat mayonnaise**
4 teaspoons **gluten-free
   mango chutney**
2 **carrots**, peeled and grated
2 **ready-cooked chicken
   breasts**, shredded
¼ small **cabbage**, thinly
   shredded
2 **tomatoes**, sliced
small handful of **coriander
   leaves**
salt and **pepper**

Lay the tortillas on a clean surface and spread
each one with 1 tablespoon of the mayonnaise and
1 tablespoon of the mango chutney.

Divide the remaining ingredients between the tortillas
and season with salt and pepper. Roll up the wraps
to serve.

For chicken club sandwiches, cook 8 unsmoked
streaky bacon rashers under a preheated hot grill
for 3–4 minutes on each side until crisp. Toast
12 slices of gluten-free bread for 2–3 minutes on each
side. Spread 4 slices of the toast with 2 tablespoons
gluten-free reduced-fat mayonnaise. Top the slices
with some shredded iceberg lettuce, 3 sliced tomatoes
and the bacon. Spread 4 more slices of toast with
2 tablespoons gluten-free mango chutney and place
on top of the bacon. Cover the mango with 2 sliced
ready-cooked chicken breasts and 1 thinly sliced small
red onion. Top with the remaining slices of toast and
secure each sandwich with 2 cocktail sticks. Slice in
half diagonally to serve. **Calories per serving 457**

beef olives

Calories per serving **340**
Serves **4**
Preparation time **15 minutes**
Cooking time **2¼ hours**

1 tablespoon **olive oil**
2 **onions**, chopped
4 **mushrooms**, chopped
2 **streaky bacon rashers**,
　chopped
1 **garlic clove**, chopped
1 teaspoon **thyme leaves**,
　chopped
4 **topside steaks**, about
　150 g (5 oz) each
1 tablespoon **gluten-free**
　Dijon mustard
2 **carrots**, peeled and diced
2 **celery sticks**, diced
400 ml (14 fl oz) **gluten-free**
　beef stock
200 ml (7 fl oz) **red wine**
steamed **cabbage** and
　carrots, to serve

Heat half the oil in a frying pan, add half the onion, the mushrooms, bacon and garlic and fry for 3–4 minutes until softened. Stir in the thyme leaves.

Spread each steak with a quarter of the mustard, then divide the stuffing mixture between them, roll up and secure with kitchen string.

Heat the remaining oil in a flameproof casserole and brown the beef rolls on all sides, then remove from the pan and set aside. Add the remaining onion, the carrots and celery to the pan and cook for 3–4 minutes, then return the beef to the pan with the stock and wine. Bring to a simmer, cover and cook over a low heat for 2 hours.

Serve with steamed cabbage and carrots.

For serious beef sandwiches, cut 2 red onions into wedges, then toss with 1 tablespoon olive oil and 1 teaspoon cumin seeds. Place in a roasting tin and roast in a preheated oven, 200°C (400°F), Gas Mark 6, for 20–25 minutes until starting to char at the edges. Cook 4 x 150 g (5 oz) sirloin steaks in a hot griddle pan until cooked to your liking. Spread 4 thick slices of gluten-free bread with 1 teaspoon gluten-free horseradish sauce each. Top each one with a small handful of rocket leaves. Place the steaks on top, then divide the roasted red onion wedges between them and top with another 4 slices of bread. Serve with homemade chips, if liked. **Calories per serving 465 (not including chips)**

teriyaki chicken salad

Calories per serving **320**
Serves **4**
Preparation time **20 minutes,
   plus marinating**
Cooking time **20–25 minutes**

4 **boneless, skinless chicken
   breasts**, about 125 g (4 oz)
   each
2 tablespoons **sunflower oil**
4 tablespoons **gluten-free soy
   sauce**
2 **garlic cloves**, finely chopped
2.5 cm (1 inch) piece of **fresh
   root ginger**, peeled and
   finely grated
2 tablespoons **sesame seeds**
2 tablespoons **sunflower
   seeds**
2 tablespoons **pumpkin
   seeds**
juice of **2 limes**
100 g (3½ oz) **herb salad**
½ small **iceberg lettuce**, torn
   into bite-sized pieces
50 g (2 oz) **alfalfa** or **broccoli
   sprouting seeds**

Put the chicken breasts into a shallow non-metallic dish. Spoon three-quarters of the oil over the chicken, then add half the soy sauce, the garlic and ginger. Turn the chicken to coat in the mixture, cover with clingfilm and leave to marinate in the refrigerator for 30 minutes.

Heat a nonstick frying pan until hot. Lift the chicken out of the marinade, add to the pan and fry for 8–10 minutes on each side until dark brown and cooked through. Remove from the pan and set aside.

Heat the remaining oil in the pan, add the seeds and fry for 2–3 minutes until lightly toasted. Add the remaining marinade and remaining soy sauce and bring to the boil, then remove from the heat and mix in the lime juice.

Mix the herb salad, lettuce and sprouting seeds together, then divide on to 4 serving plates. Thinly slice the chicken and arrange on top. Spoon over the seed dressing and serve immediately.

For teriyaki chicken with oriental salad, marinate the chicken as above and make a salad with 200 g (7 oz) carrots, cut into thin strips, 4 spring onions, cut into thin strips, 6 thinly sliced radishes and ½ small head of Chinese leaves, thinly shredded. Fry the chicken as above, omit the seeds and then continue with the dressing as above. Slice the chicken, arrange on the salad and drizzle with the warm dressing. **Calories per serving 239**

potato drop scones

Calories per serving **399**
Serves **4**
Preparation time **10 minutes**
Cooking time **20–25 minutes**

550 g (1 lb 3 oz) **potatoes**,
  peeled and chopped
1 ½ teaspoons **gluten-free
  baking powder**
2 **eggs**
4–5 tablespoons **skimmed
  milk**
1 tablespoon **sunflower oil**
salt and **pepper**

To serve
4 **eggs**
8 **bacon rashers**

Cook the potatoes in a saucepan of boiling water for 12–15 minutes until tender. Drain, then return to the pan and mash until smooth. Beat in the baking powder, eggs and enough of the milk to form a smooth mixture the consistency of thick cream. Season well.

Heat the oil in a frying pan and drop in heaped dessertspoons of the mixture. Cook for 3–4 minutes, turning once, until golden brown. Remove from the pan and keep warm. Repeat with the remaining mixture.

Meanwhile, bring a saucepan of water to a gentle simmer and stir with a large spoon to create a swirl. Break 2 eggs into the water and cook for 3–4 minutes. Remove with a slotted spoon and keep warm. Repeat with the remaining eggs.

Cook the bacon under a preheated hot grill for 5–6 minutes, or until crisp.

Serve the drop scones with the bacon and poached eggs.

baked sole with fennel pesto

Calories per serving **370**
Serves **4**
Preparation time **20 minutes**
Cooking time **15 minutes**

1 **fennel bulb**, roughly
    chopped
2 tablespoons chopped **dill**
50 g (2 oz) **toasted pine nuts**
2 tablespoons **ground
    almonds**
50 g (2 oz) **Parmesan
    cheese**, grated
juice of ½ **lemon**
100 ml (3½ fl oz) **olive oil**,
    plus 1 tablespoon for
    drizzling
4 **lemon sole fillets**, about
    175 g (6 oz) each, skinned
2 **courgettes**
200 g (7 oz) **green beans**
2 **tomatoes**, chopped

Place the fennel in a blender or food processor
and blend to a purée. Add the dill, pine nuts, ground
almonds, cheese and lemon juice and blitz to combine.
With the motor still running, slowly pour in the 100 ml
(3½ fl oz) olive oil through the feed tube until combined.

Lay the sole fillets on a board, skinned side up, and
spread with the fennel pesto. Using a vegetable peeler,
slice the courgettes into long, thin strips, then place
2–3 slices on each sole fillet. Roll up the fish and place
in an ovenproof dish.

Drizzle with the remaining oil, cover with foil and bake
in a preheated oven, 190°C (375°F), Gas Mark 5, for
15 minutes until cooked through.

Meanwhile, cook the green beans in a steamer, then
toss with the tomatoes and divide between 4 plates.
Top each with a sole fillet and serve.

For sole & fennel soup, heat 1 tablespoon olive oil
in a large saucepan, add 1 chopped onion and 2 sliced
garlic cloves and cook for 2 minutes until starting to
soften. Add 2 thinly sliced fennel bulbs and cook for
a further 8 minutes. Stir in 100 ml (3½ fl oz) white wine
and cook for 2 minutes, then add 500 ml (17 fl oz)
hot gluten-free fish stock, 2 x 400 g (13 oz) cans
chopped tomatoes and salt and pepper. Bring to the
boil, then reduce the heat and simmer for 5 minutes.
Add 625 g (1¼ lb) chopped skinned sole fillets and
cook for 3 minutes, or until cooked through. Stir in
2 tablespoons chopped parsley and serve with gluten-
free crusty bread. **Calories per serving 245 (not
including bread)**

mushroom chilli

Calories per serving **347**
Serves **4**
Preparation time **10 minutes**
Cooking time **15–20 minutes**

1 tablespoon **olive oil**
1 **onion**, diced
2 **red chillies**, deseeded and
  finely diced
1 **garlic clove**, crushed
2 teaspoons **ground cumin**
400 g (13 oz) **mixed
  mushrooms**, chopped
400 g (13 oz) can **chopped
  tomatoes**
1 tablespoon **tomato purée**
400 g (13 oz) can **red kidney
  beans**, rinsed and drained
2–3 tablespoons **water**
2 tablespoons chopped
  parsley
salt and **pepper**
600 g (1 ¼ lb) cooked
  basmati rice, to serve

Heat the oil in a frying pan, add the onion and fry for
2–3 minutes until starting to soften. Stir in the chillies,
garlic and cumin and cook for a further 2 minutes.

Add the mushrooms, tomatoes, tomato purée, kidney
beans and measurement water, bring to a simmer and
cook for 12–15 minutes.

Season to taste and stir in the chopped parsley, then
serve with the cooked basmati rice.

For garlic mushrooms on toast, heat 1 tablespoon
olive oil in a frying pan, add 400 g (13 oz) sliced
chestnut mushrooms and fry for 4–5 minutes until
softened. Add 2 finely chopped garlic cloves and
cook for 1 minute, then stir in 2 tablespoons crème
fraîche. Meanwhile, toast 4 thick slices of gluten-free
bread. Season the mushrooms to taste and pour over
the toast. Serve sprinkled with 1 tablespoon chopped
parsley. **Calories per serving 200**

pork, apple & ginger stir-fry

Calories per serving **357**
Serves **4**
Preparation time **15 minutes**
Cooking time **12–15 minutes**

2 tablespoons **sesame seeds**
1 tablespoon **coconut oil**
300 g (10 oz) **pork fillet**, in
  strips
2 **garlic cloves**, chopped
5 cm (2 inch) piece of **fresh
  root ginger**, peeled and cut
  into matchsticks
1 **green chilli**, deseeded and
  chopped
2 **apples**, cored and cut into
  wedges
2 **carrots**, peeled and cut into
  matchsticks
150 g (5 oz) **broccoli florets**
300 g (10 oz) **ribbon rice
  noodles**
juice of **1 lime**

Heat a nonstick frying pan over a medium-low heat
and dry-fry the sesame seeds for 2 minutes, stirring
frequently, until golden and toasted. Set aside.

Heat the oil in a wok or large frying pan, add the pork
and stir-fry for 6–8 minutes until lightly browned.
Add the garlic, ginger, chilli, apples and vegetables
and stir-fry for a further 4–5 minutes, or until the pork
is cooked through.

Meanwhile, cook the noodles according to the packet
instructions, then add to the stir-fry with the lime juice
and toss all the ingredients together.

Serve sprinkled with the toasted sesame seeds.

For grilled pork steaks with apple & ginger
coleslaw, cook 4 x 150 g (5 oz) pork steaks under
a preheated hot grill for 3–4 minutes on each side,
or until cooked through. Meanwhile, finely slice
1 small white cabbage, 2 celery sticks and 1 cored
and deseeded red pepper and place in a bowl. Add
2 peeled and grated carrots and 2 peeled, cored and
grated apples and mix well. Mix together 2 tablespoons
natural yogurt, a 2.5 cm (1 inch) piece of fresh root
ginger, peeled and grated, and 1 tablespoon gluten-free
mayonnaise in a small bowl, then stir into the coleslaw
with 2 tablespoons chopped coriander. Serve with the
grilled pork. **Calories per serving 386**

roasted veggie & quinoa salad

Calories per serving **372**
Serves **4**
Preparation time **5 minutes**
Cooking time **20–25 minutes**

3 **courgettes**, cut into chunks
2 **red peppers**, cored,
   deseeded and cut into
   chunks
2 **red onions**, cut into wedges
1 large **aubergine**, cut into
   chunks
3 **garlic cloves**, peeled
3 tablespoons **olive oil**
150 g (5 oz) **quinoa**
2 tablespoons **green pesto** or
   sun-dried tomato paste
1 tablespoon **balsamic
   vinegar**
75 g (3 oz) **rocket leaves**

Put all the vegetables and garlic on a large baking
sheet and drizzle over the olive oil. Place in a preheated
oven, 220°C (425°F), Gas Mark 7, for 20–25 minutes
until tender and beginning to char.

Meanwhile, cook the quinoa in a saucepan of boiling
water according to the packet instructions, then
drain well.

Whisk together the pesto or tomato paste and balsamic
vinegar in a small bowl. Place the roasted vegetables,
rocket and quinoa in a large serving bowl and stir in the
dressing. Serve warm.

For quinoa with salmon & watercress, cook the
quinoa as above. Meanwhile, place 2 large pieces of
skinless salmon fillet, about 300 g (10 oz) in total, in
a nonstick frying pan and cook for 3 minutes on each
side until crisp and just cooked through, then flake.
Whisk together 200 g (7 oz) light crème fraîche, the
grated rind and juice of 1 orange and 1 tablespoon
gluten-free wholegrain mustard in a small bowl. Stir
the dressing into the quinoa with the flaked salmon
and a bunch of chopped watercress. **Calories per
serving 381**

mackerel curry

Calories per serving **381**
Serves **4**
Preparation time **10 minutes**
Cooking time **15–20 minutes**

1 **green chilli**, deseeded and
  chopped
1 teaspoon **ground coriander**
½ teaspoon **turmeric**
4 **garlic cloves**
2.5 cm (1 inch) piece of **fresh
  root ginger**, peeled and
  sliced
1 teaspoon **sunflower oil**
1 tablespoon **coconut oil**
1 teaspoon **cumin seeds**
1 large **onion**, sliced
150 ml (¼ pint) **coconut milk**
250 ml (8 fl oz) **water**
450 g (14½ oz) **mackerel
  fillets**, cut into 5 cm (2 inch)
  pieces
small handful of **coriander
  leaves**, roughly torn
salt and **pepper**

Place the chilli, ground coriander, turmeric, garlic, ginger
and sunflower oil in a blender or food processor and
blend together to make a smooth paste.

Heat the coconut oil in a wok or frying pan over a
medium heat, add the spice paste and the cumin seeds
and cook for 2–3 minutes.

Add the onion to the pan and cook for 1–2 minutes,
then pour in the coconut milk and measurement water.
Bring to the boil, then reduce the heat and simmer for
5 minutes. Season with salt and pepper.

Add the mackerel pieces to the pan and cook for
6–8 minutes until the fish is cooked through, then
stir in the coriander leaves.

For mackerel, beetroot & horseradish salad, cut
425 g (14 oz) raw beetroot into 4–6 wedges, place in
a roasting tin with 2 tablespoons olive oil, 2 teaspoons
cumin seeds, 2 tablespoons thyme and 2 teaspoons
clear honey and mix to coat. Roast in a preheated
oven, 200°C (400°F), Gas Mark 6, for 25 minutes
until tender. Meanwhile, whisk together 2 tablespoons
gluten-free creamed horseradish, 4 tablespoons lemon
juice and 150 ml (¼ pint) low-fat natural yogurt in a
small bowl. Heat 4 x 85 g (3 oz) smoked mackerel
fillets according to the packet instructions, then flake
into large flakes. Place a few small handfuls of baby
spinach leaves on to 4 plates and scatter over the
mackerel and beetroot. Sprinkle with the horseradish
dressing and serve. **Calories per serving 412**

granola

Calories per serving **305**
Serves **4**
Preparation time **5 minutes,**
  plus cooling
Cooking time **20 minutes**

½ tablespoon **sunflower oil**
1 tablespoon **maple syrup**
½ tablespoon **clear honey**
75 g (3 oz) **gluten-free rolled**
  oats
15 g (½ oz) **sunflower seeds**
1 tablespoon **sesame seeds**
15 g (½ oz) **pumpkin seeds**
25 g (1 oz) **flaked almonds**
25 g (1 oz) **dried cranberries**
15 g (½ oz) **desiccated**
  coconut

To serve
400 g (13 oz) **natural yogurt**
320 g (11 oz) **strawberries,**
  hulled and halved if large

Mix together the oil, maple syrup and honey in a bowl, then add the oats, seeds and almonds and mix well.

Spread the mixture over a baking sheet and bake in a preheated oven, 120°C (250°F), Gas Mark ½, for 10 minutes. Stir in the cranberries and coconut, then return to the oven and cook for a further 10 minutes – keep an eye on the mixture as nuts and seeds can burn very easily.

Spoon on to a tray and leave to cool, then divide between 4 bowls and serve with the yogurt and strawberries.

For bircher muesli, mix together 75 g (3 oz) gluten-free rolled oats, 75 ml (3 fl oz) apple juice, a large pinch each of ground cinnamon and nutmeg, 1 grated dessert apple, 1 tablespoon chopped pecan nuts, 1 tablespoon dried cranberries and 150 ml (¼ pint) water in a large bowl. Cover and leave to soak overnight in the refrigerator. Stir in 2 tablespoons low-fat natural yogurt, divide into 4 bowls and serve sprinkled with 2 tablespoons fresh raspberries. **Calories per serving 211**

blueberry pancakes

Calories per serving **363**
Serves **4**
Preparation time **5 minutes**
Cooking time **10–15 minutes**

125 g (4 oz) **gluten-free self-
raising flour**
1 teaspoon **gluten-free
baking powder**
1 **egg**
150 ml (¼ pint) **soya milk**
25 g (1 oz) **unsalted butter**,
melted
100 g (3½ oz) **blueberries**
1 tablespoon **olive oil**

To serve
4 tablespoons **crème fraîche**
4 teaspoons **maple syrup**

Mix together the flour and baking powder in a large
bowl. Whisk together the egg and milk in a jug, then
pour into the dry ingredients and whisk until smooth.
Whisk in the melted butter, then stir in 75 g (3 oz) of
the blueberries.

Heat the oil in a frying pan over a medium heat, then
spoon tablespoons of the mixture into the pan. Cook
for 3–4 minutes until golden underneath, then flip the
pancakes over and cook for a further 2–3 minutes.
Remove from the pan and keep warm. Repeat with the
remaining batter.

Serve with the remaining blueberries, dollops of crème
fraîche and a drizzle of maple syrup.

For blueberry smoothies, place 750 ml (1¼ pints)
apple juice, 400 g (13 oz) natural yogurt, 3 chopped
bananas and 500 g (1 lb) blueberries in a blender or
food processor and blend until smooth, adding a little
milk if too thick. Pour into 4 glasses to serve. **Calories
per serving 258**

sweet french toast with berries

Calories per serving **370**
Serves **4**
Preparation time **15 minutes**
Cooking time **4–6 minutes**

2 **oranges**
400 g (13 oz) **fat-free Greek yogurt**
100 g (3½ oz) **blueberries**
100 g (3½ oz) **strawberries**, hulled and quartered
2 **eggs**, beaten
50 g (2 oz) **caster sugar**
2 tablespoons **sesame seeds**
pinch of **ground cinnamon**
25 g (1 oz) **unsalted butter**
4 slices of **gluten-free bread**

Grate the rind of the oranges, then stir into the yogurt and chill. Segment the oranges over a bowl to catch the juice.

Place the blueberries and strawberries in bowl. Add the orange segments and pour over the juice.

Whisk together the eggs, sugar, sesame seeds and ground cinnamon in a shallow bowl.

Melt the butter in a large frying pan over a medium heat. Dip the slices of bread into the egg mixture, then transfer to the pan and cook for 2–3 minutes on each side until golden.

Serve each slice of French toast topped with a quarter of the fruit and a dollop of the yogurt, with the juices poured over.

For warm berry compote & yogurt, place 125 g (4 oz) raspberries, 125 g (4 oz) blueberries and 200 g (7 oz) hulled and halved strawberries in a small saucepan with 2 tablespoons clear honey and heat through for 6–7 minutes, stirring occasionally. Divide 500 g (1 lb) fat-free Greek yogurt between 4 small bowls or glasses and pour over the warm compote. Serve immediately. **Calories per serving 145**

hazelnut, chocolate & pear cake

Calories per serving **319 (not including crème fraîche)**
Serves **8**
Preparation time **20 minutes, plus cooling**
Cooking time **45 minutes**

85 g (3 oz) **butter**, diced, plus extra for greasing
85 g (3 oz) **gluten-free plain dark chocolate**, broken into pieces
1 tablespoon **Amaretto liqueur**
3 **eggs**, separated
85 g (3 oz) **caster sugar**
85 g (3 oz) **hazelnuts**, toasted and ground
3 **pears**, peeled, halved and cored
icing sugar, for dusting

Grease a 25 cm (10 inch) loose-bottomed cake tin with butter and line the base with nonstick baking paper.

Melt the butter and chocolate in a heatproof bowl set over a pan of gently simmering water, making sure the bottom of the bowl does not touch the water. Remove from the heat, stir in the Amaretto and leave to cool.

Whisk the egg yolks and sugar in a bowl until pale and thick. Fold into the chocolate mixture with the ground hazelnuts. Whisk the egg whites in a separate clean bowl until soft peaks form, then carefully fold 2 tablespoons of the mixture into the chocolate mixture. Repeat until all the whites are folded in.

Spoon the mixture into the prepared tin and level the top. Arrange the pear halves over the mixture, cut side down.

Bake in a preheated oven, 180°C (350°F), Gas Mark 4, for 40 minutes until the pears are soft and the cake is cooked through. Leave to cool slightly in the tin, then turn out on to a wire rack and leave to cool completely.

Dust with icing sugar and serve with low-fat crème fraîche, if liked.

chocolate cake

Calories per serving **392**
Serves **6**
Preparation time **5 minutes**
Cooking time **35–40 minutes**

75 g (3 oz) **coconut oil**,
  melted, plus extra for
  greasing
400 g (13 oz) can **kidney
  beans**, rinsed and drained
100 g (3½ oz) **rice flour**
50 g (2 oz) **gluten-free cocoa
  powder**, plus extra for sifting
1½ teaspoons **gluten-free
  baking powder**
125 g (4 oz) **light muscovado
  sugar**
3 large **eggs**
raspberries, to serve

Grease a 20 cm (8 inch) spring-form cake tin with coconut oil and line the base with nonstick baking paper.

Place all the ingredients in a food processor or blender and blitz to a smooth batter, then spoon the mixture into the prepared tin.

Bake in a preheated oven, 180°C (350°F), Gas Mark 4, for 35–40 minutes until a skewer inserted into the centre comes out clean. Leave to cool slightly in the tin, then turn out on to a wire rack and leave to cool completely before serving.

Sift with cocoa powder and serve with a few raspberries.

For chocolate mousse, melt 225 g (7½ oz) chopped gluten-free plain dark chocolate in a heatproof bowl set over a pan of gently simmering water, making sure the bottom of the bowl does not touch the water. Add 10 g (⅓ oz) butter, 1 tablespoon brandy (optional) and 3 large egg yolks, one at a time, stirring until combined. Leave to cool slightly. Whisk 3 egg whites in a large clean bowl until just stiff. In a separate bowl, beat 150 ml (¼ pint) double cream until lightly whipped, then fold the cream and egg whites into the chocolate mixture. Spoon into 6 small glasses or ramekins and chill for at least 1 hour before serving. **Calories per serving 383**

caramelized autumn fruits

Calories per serving **309**
Serves **4**
Preparation time **10 minutes**
Cooking time **15–20 minutes**

60 g (2¼ oz) **butter**
60 g (2¼ oz) **golden caster
    sugar**
juice of **1 orange**
3 **dessert apples**, peeled,
    cored and quartered
3 **pears**, peeled, cored and
    quartered
4 **plums**, halved and stoned

Heat the butter in a large frying pan, add the sugar and orange juice and cook, stirring, until the sugar dissolves. Increase the heat and cook for 6–8 minutes until the mixture turns golden.

Add the apples and pears and stir into the caramel. Cook for 4–5 minutes until they start to soften.

Stir in the plums and cook for a further 4–5 minutes until all the fruit is soft and coated in caramel. Serve warm.

For autumn fruit compote, place 2 cored and sliced apples, 2 cored and sliced pears, 4 halved and stoned plums, 6 ready-to-eat dried apricots, 6 pitted prunes, the juice of 2 oranges, 2 tablespoons clear honey, 3 cloves and 1 cinnamon stick in a large saucepan and bring to the boil, then reduce the heat and simmer for 8–9 minutes. Spoon into 4 bowls and top each with 40 g (1½ oz) thick natural yogurt. Serve sprinkled with ground nutmeg. **Calories per serving 246**

blackberry & apple crumbles

Calories per serving **358**
Serves **4**
Preparation time **10 minutes**
Cooking time **22–25 minutes**

4 **dessert apples**, peeled,
   cored and thinly sliced
125 g (4 oz) **blackberries**
2 teaspoons **caster sugar**
100 g (3½ oz) **gluten-free
   rolled oats**
50 g (2 oz) **unsalted butter**,
   diced
40 g (1½ oz) **dark
   muscovado sugar**
25 g (1 oz) **flaked almonds**

Divide the apple slices and blackberries between 4 small ovenproof dishes or ramekins and sprinkle with the caster sugar.

Place the oats, butter, muscovado sugar and almonds in a food processor and blitz until the mixture resembles breadcrumbs. Spoon the oat mixture over the fruit.

Bake in a preheated oven, 190°C (375°F), Gas Mark 5, for 22–25 minutes until golden.

For blackberry & apple fool, whip 300 ml (½ pint) double cream until soft peaks form. Gently fold in 150 g (5 oz) unsweetened stewed apple and 125 oz (4 oz) lightly crushed blackberries. Divide between 4 glasses and chill until ready to serve. **Calories per serving 416**

very berry & fromage frais fool

Calories per serving **313**
Serves **4**
Preparation time **5 minutes,**
   plus cooling and chilling
Cooking time **5 minutes**

3 tablespoons **crème de
   cassis** or **spiced red fruit
   cordial**
250 g (8 oz) **mixed frozen
   berries**
2–4 tablespoons **icing sugar**
500 g (1 lb) **fat-free fromage
   frais**
250 g (8 oz) **low-fat
   blackcurrant yogurt**
1 **vanilla pod**, split in half
   lengthways
4 tablespoons **toasted flaked
   almonds**, to serve

Put the crème de cassis or cordial in a saucepan over a low heat and gently heat, then add the berries. Stir, cover and cook for about 5 minutes, or until the fruit has defrosted and is beginning to collapse. Remove from the heat and stir in 1–3 tablespoons of the icing sugar, according to taste. Cool completely, then chill for at least 1 hour.

Mix together the fromage frais, yogurt and 1 tablespoon of the icing sugar in a bowl. Scrape in the seeds from the vanilla pod and beat to combine.

Fold the berries into the fromage frais mixture until just combined. Carefully spoon into 4 decorative glasses or glass serving dishes and serve immediately, scattered with the toasted almonds.

For exotic fruit fool, replace the crème de cassis with 3 tablespoons coconut cream and the mixed berries with 250 g (8 oz) exotic fruit mix and add 1 tablespoon lime juice. Heat as above, then blend in a food processor or blender until smooth. Chill as above. Mix the fromage frais with 2 tablespoons coconut cream and 250 g (8 oz) low-fat mango yogurt instead of the blackcurrant yogurt. Fold in the fruit purée and serve sprinkled with 4 tablespoons toasted coconut flakes. **Calories per serving 313**

recipes
under 500
calories

grilled salmon with kale salad

Calories per serving **463**
Serves **4**
Preparation time **15 minutes**
Cooking time **8–11 minutes**

1 tablespoon **sunflower
seeds**
200 g (7 oz) **kale**, shredded
4 **salmon fillets**, about 150 g
(5 oz) each
¼ small **red cabbage**,
shredded
1 **carrot**, peeled and cut into
matchsticks
1 **avocado**, peeled, stoned
and sliced
100 g (3½ oz) **cherry
tomatoes**, halved
2 tablespoons **extra virgin
olive oil**
juice of ½ **lime**
½ teaspoon **gluten-free Dijon
mustard**
½ teaspoon **maple syrup**
2 tablespoons chopped
chives
pepper

Heat a nonstick frying pan over a medium-low heat and
dry-fry the sunflower seeds for 2–3 minutes, stirring
frequently, until slightly golden and toasted. Set aside.

Place the kale in a colander, then pour over boiling
water to slightly wilt the kale. Refresh under cold
running water and drain.

Cook the salmon fillets under a preheated hot grill for
3–4 minutes on each side, or until cooked through.

Meanwhile, toss the kale together with the cabbage,
carrot, avocado and tomatoes in a serving bowl. Whisk
together the remaining ingredients and pour over
the salad.

Scatter the toasted seeds over the salad. Serve the
salad with the salmon and sprinkle over a little pepper.

For Chinese-style kale with pan-fried tuna, heat
1 tablespoon sunflower oil in a wok and stir-fry 2 sliced
garlic cloves for a few seconds, then add 200 g (7 oz)
shredded kale. Toss around in the garlicky oil, then
pour over 100 ml (3½ fl oz) boiling water and cook for
5–6 minutes until the kale has wilted. Meanwhile, heat
1 tablespoon olive oil in a separate frying pan and cook
4 x 150 g (5 oz) tuna steaks for 3–4 minutes on each
side (depending on how rare you like your tuna). Stir
1 tablespoon gluten-free soy sauce and 1 tablespoon
gluten-free oyster sauce into the kale and heat through.
Serve topped with the tuna. **Calories per serving 288**

orange & prawn noodle salad

Calories per serving **459**
Serves **4**
Preparation time **10 minutes**
Cooking time **5 minutes**

2 tablespoons **sesame seeds**
300 g (10 oz) **rice noodles**
2 **oranges**
300 g (10 oz) **cooked peeled
   king prawns**
100 g (3½ oz) **watercress**
1 **red onion**, finely sliced
3 tablespoons **gluten-free
   sweet chilli dipping sauce**
juice of **1 lime**
2 **Little Gem lettuces**, leaves
   separated

Heat a nonstick frying pan over a medium-low heat and dry-fry the sesame seeds for 2 minutes, stirring frequently, until golden brown and toasted. Set aside.

Cook the rice noodles according to the packet instructions, then refresh under cold running water.

Segment the oranges over a bowl to catch the juice. Transfer the noodles to a large bowl, add the orange segments, prawns, watercress and onion and mix together.

Add the sweet chilli sauce and lime juice to the orange juice and whisk together. Pour over the noodle mixture and toss together.

Arrange the lettuce leaves on a large serving plate or 4 individual plates and top with the noodle salad. Sprinkle with the toasted sesame seeds and serve.

For prawn cocktail, mix together the grated rind of 1 orange, 4 tablespoons gluten-free mayonnaise and 1 tablespoon gluten-free tomato ketchup in a small bowl. Shred ½ small iceberg lettuce and divide between 4 glass bowls. Top with 400 g (13 oz) cooked peeled prawns, then pour over the mayonnaise. Serve sprinkled with 1 tablespoon toasted flaked almonds and 1 tablespoon chopped coriander. **Calories per serving 237**

smoked mackerel superfood salad

Calories per serving **492**
Serves **4**
Preparation time **15 minutes**
Cooking time **20 minutes**

500 g (1 lb) **butternut
squash**, peeled, deseeded
and cut into 1 cm (½ inch)
cubes
3 tablespoons **olive oil**
1 teaspoon **cumin seeds**
1 head of **broccoli**, cut into
florets
200 g (7 oz) **frozen** or **fresh
peas**
3 tablespoons **quinoa**
3 tablespoons **mixed seeds**
2 **smoked mackerel fillets**
juice of **1 lemon**
½ teaspoon **clear honey**
½ teaspoon **gluten-free Dijon
mustard**
100 g (3½ oz) **red cabbage**,
shredded
4 **tomatoes**, chopped
4 **ready-cooked fresh
beetroots**, cut into wedges
20 g (¾ oz) **radish sprouts**

Place the squash in a roasting tin and sprinkle with
1 tablespoon of the oil and the cumin seeds. Place
in a preheated oven, 200°C (400°F), Gas Mark 6, for
15–18 minutes until tender. Leave to cool slightly.

Meanwhile, cook the broccoli in a saucepan of boiling
water for 4–5 minutes until tender, adding the peas
3 minutes before the end of the cooking time. Remove
with a slotted spoon and refresh under cold running
water, then drain. Cook the quinoa in the broccoli water
for 15 minutes, or according to the packet instructions,
then drain and leave to cool slightly.

Heat a nonstick frying pan over a medium-low heat and
dry-fry the seeds, stirring frequently, until golden brown.
Set aside. Heat the mackerel fillets according to the
packet instructions, then skin and break into flakes.

Whisk together the remaining oil, lemon juice, honey
and mustard in a small bowl. Toss together all the
ingredients, except the radish sprouts, with the dressing
in a serving bowl. Serve topped with the sprouts.

For smoked mackerel superfood soup, heat
1 tablespoon oil in a saucepan and fry 1 chopped
onion and 1 crushed garlic clove for 3–4 minutes. Add
625 g (1¼ lb) peeled, deseeded and diced butternut
squash, 100 g (3½ oz) broccoli florets, 2 tablespoons
quinoa, 600 ml (1 pint) gluten-free vegetable stock
and 150 ml (¼ pint) orange juice and simmer for
15 minutes. Blend until smooth. Stir in 2 skinned, flaked
smoked mackerel fillets and cook for 1 minute. Serve
sprinkled with 2 tablespoons toasted pumpkin seeds.
Calories per serving 416

parsnip, lentil & walnut salad

Calories per serving **435**
Serves **4**
Preparation time **10 minutes**
Cooking time **30–35 minutes**

4 **parsnips**, peeled and cut
  into batons
4 tablespoons **olive oil**
30 g (1 oz) **walnuts**
750 ml (1¼ pints) **gluten-free**
  vegetable stock
200 g (7 oz) **Puy lentils**
juice of ½ **lemon**
1 teaspoon **clear honey**
½ teaspoon **gluten-free**
  wholegrain mustard
½ **garlic clove**, crushed
25 g (1 oz) **watercress**
25 g (1 oz) **rocket leaves**
25 g (1 oz) **baby spinach**
  leaves
20 g (¾ oz) **Parmesan**
  cheese shavings

Place the parsnips in a roasting tin and drizzle with 1 tablespoon of the oil. Roast in a preheated oven, 200°C (400°F), Gas Mark 6, for 30–35 minutes until golden, adding the walnuts 5 minutes before the end of the cooking time.

Meanwhile, bring the stock to the boil in a saucepan, add the lentils and cook for 25–30 minutes until the lentils are just tender. Drain.

Whisk together the remaining oil, lemon juice, honey, mustard and garlic in a small bowl.

Transfer the lentils, walnuts and parsnips to a serving bowl, then toss together with the dressing and salad leaves. Serve topped with Parmesan shavings.

For curried parsnip & lentil soup, heat 1 tablespoon olive oil in a saucepan, add 3 peeled and chopped parsnips and cook for 2–3 minutes. Stir in 1 teaspoon curry powder and 50 g (2 oz) red lentils and cook for 1 minute, then stir in 900 ml (1½ pints) gluten-free vegetable stock. Simmer for 20–25 minutes until the parsnips are tender. Remove from the heat and blend with a hand-hand blender, adding a little milk to loosen if needed. Ladle into 4 bowls and serve sprinkled with 1 tablespoon chopped toasted walnuts and ½ tablespoon grated Parmesan cheese. **Calories per serving 198**

spicy tomato tagliatelle

Calories per serving **442**
Serves **4**
Preparation time **5 minutes**
Cooking time **10 minutes**

½ tablespoon **olive oil**
1 **red chilli**, deseeded and
  diced
5 cm (2 inch) piece of **fresh
  root ginger**, peeled and
  grated
3 **garlic cloves**, finely sliced
400 g (13 oz) can **chopped
  tomatoes**
1 teaspoon **sugar**
3–4 **anchovy fillets** in oil,
  drained
2 tablespoons chopped
  parsley
400 g (13 oz) **gluten-free
  dried tagliatelle**
salt and **pepper**
2 tablespoons grated **Cheddar
  cheese**, to serve

Heat the oil in a frying pan, add the chilli and ginger and cook for 1 minute, then add the garlic and cook for a further 1 minute.

Pour in the tomatoes, stir in the sugar and anchovies and bring to a simmer. Cook for 5–6 minutes. Add the parsley and season to taste.

Meanwhile, cook the tagliatelle in a saucepan of boiling water according to the packet instructions. Drain and return to the pan, then pour in the sauce and toss together well.

Serve sprinkled with the grated cheese.

For spicy tomato soup, heat 1 tablespoon olive oil in a saucepan, add 2 chopped onions, 1 peeled and chopped carrot and 3 cored, deseeded and chopped red peppers and cook for 10–12 minutes until softened. Add 3 sliced garlic cloves and 1 sliced red chilli and cook for a further 2–3 minutes. Pour in a 400 g (13 oz) can chopped tomatoes and 850 ml (1½ pints) gluten-free vegetable stock and bring to the boil, then reduce the heat and simmer for 10–15 minutes. Blend using a hand-hand blender, then season. Ladle into 4 bowls and serve with a drizzle of olive oil and sprinkling of pepper. **Calories per serving 163**

prawn & spinach curry

Calories per serving **474**
Serves **4**
Preparation time **10 minutes**
Cooking time **12–15 minutes**

4 **tomatoes**
2 tablespoons **groundnut oil**
2 **red onions**, chopped
2.5 cm (1 inch) piece of **fresh root ginger**, peeled and grated
4 **garlic cloves**, sliced
¼ teaspoon **chilli powder**
½ teaspoon **turmeric**
1 teaspoon **ground coriander**
400 ml (14 fl oz) can **reduced-fat coconut milk**
150 g (5 oz) **spinach**, chopped
425 g (14 oz) **raw peeled king prawns**
1 tablespoon **toasted flaked almonds**
600 g (1¼ lb) **cooked basmati rice**, to serve

Place the tomatoes in a heatproof bowl and pour over boiling water to cover. Leave for 1–2 minutes, then drain, cut a cross at the stem end of each tomato and peel off the skins and chop.

Heat the oil in a wok or large frying pan, add the onions, ginger and garlic and stir-fry for 2–3 minutes. Add the spices and cook for a further 2–3 minutes, then add the tomatoes. Pour in the coconut milk and bring to a simmer. Gradually add the spinach, stirring until wilted. Cook for 4–5 minutes.

Stir in the prawns and cook for a further 2 minutes, or until the prawns turn pink and are cooked through. Sprinkle with the almonds and serve with the cooked rice.

For prawn & spinach soufflés, heat 1 tablespoon olive oil in a pan, add 225 g (7½ oz) baby spinach leaves and cook for 2–3 minutes until wilted. Meanwhile, melt 45 g (1½ oz) butter in a saucepan, then stir in 45 g (1½ oz) gluten-free plain flour to make a roux. Gradually whisk in 350 ml (12 fl oz) milk and cook, stirring continuously, for 2–3 minutes until the sauce is thick and smooth. Stir in 50 g (2 oz) grated Parmesan cheese, season and pour into a large bowl. Stir in the spinach and leave to cool for 3–4 minutes. Put 3 cooked peeled king prawns in each of 4 greased ramekins, then place on a baking sheet. Whisk 4 egg yolks into the spinach sauce. Whisk 4 egg whites in a large clean bowl until stiff, then gently fold into the spinach mixture. Spoon into the ramekins, running a finger around the rim to help even rising. Sprinkle over 2 tablespoons grated Parmesan cheese and bake in a preheated oven, 200°C (400°F), Gas Mark 6, for 20 minutes until risen and golden. **Calories per serving 386**

roasted salmon & vegetables

Calories per serving **457**
Serves **4**
Preparation time **15 minutes**
Cooking time **40–45 minutes**

600 g (1 ¼ lb) **sweet
  potatoes**, peeled and cut
  into wedges
1 large **fennel bulb**, cut into
  8 wedges
2 **garlic cloves**, chopped
small bunch of **parsley**,
  chopped
2 tablespoons **olive oil**
1 tablespoon chopped **mint**
4 **salmon fillets**, about 125 g
  (4 oz) each, skin scored
  3 times
grated rind and juice of 1
  lemon
pepper

To serve
25 g (1 oz) **Parmesan cheese**
  shavings
lemon wedges

Cook the sweet potatoes and fennel in a saucepan of boiling water for 4 minutes, then drain. Transfer to a roasting tin and sprinkle with the garlic, pepper, half the parsley and the olive oil. Toss together. Roast in a preheated oven, 220°C (425°F), Gas Mark 7, for 20–25 minutes until the vegetables are tender and golden.

Meanwhile, rub the remaining parsley and the mint into the scored salmon skin. Set aside.

Lay the salmon, skin side up, on top of the vegetables, sprinkle with the lemon rind and juice and roast for a further 15 minutes, or until the fish is cooked through and the vegetables are tender.

Sprinkle with the Parmesan shavings and serve with lemon wedges.

For fennel & salmon soup, heat 1 tablespoon olive oil in a pan, add 2 chopped shallots and fry for 2–3 minutes. Add 400 g (13 oz) new potatoes and 2 chopped fennel bulbs and cook for a further 3–4 minutes. Pour in 900 ml (1 ½ pints) gluten-free vegetable stock and simmer for 10–12 minutes until the vegetables are tender. Blend with a hand-hand blender, then return to the heat, season and drop in 400 g (13 oz) skinless salmon fillet, cut into chunks, and cook for 3–4 minutes until the fish is cooked through. Ladle into 4 bowls and serve sprinkled with chopped parsley. **Calories per serving 325**

beetroot & goats' cheese risotto

Calories per serving **451**
Serves **4**
Preparation time **10 minutes**
Cooking time **25 minutes**

½ tablespoon **olive oil**
1 large **onion**, chopped
1 litre (1¾ pints) **gluten-free vegetable stock**
100 ml (3½ fl oz) **water**
400 g (13 oz) **ready-cooked fresh beetroot**, coarsely grated
2 **garlic cloves**, peeled and chopped
300 g (10 oz) **risotto rice**
100 ml (3½ fl oz) **red wine**
1 tablespoon grated **Parmesan cheese**
2 tablespoons chopped **dill**
75 g (3 oz) **goats' cheese**, chopped
salt and **pepper**

Heat the oil in a saucepan, add the onion and fry for 5 minutes until softened.

Meanwhile, pour the stock and measurement water into a separate saucepan, add half the beetroot and gently heat.

Add the garlic to the onion and cook for a further 1 minute, then stir in the rice. Pour over the wine and allow it to sizzle. When the liquid is reduced, add a ladle of the hot beetroot stock and stir. Continue to cook and stir until the liquid has been absorbed, then repeat with another ladle of stock. Continue cooking until almost all of the stock is used and the rice is al dente.

Stir in the remaining grated beetroot and cook, stirring, until the risotto is creamy.

Add the Parmesan and dill, season to taste, then divide between 4 bowls. Top with the goats' cheese and serve.

For beetroot & goats' cheese salad, cook 4 raw beetroots in a saucepan of salted boiling water for 30–40 minutes until tender. Drain, then peel off the skins. Cut each beetroot into wedges and toss in a salad bowl with 250 g (8 oz) crumbled goats' cheese, 75 g (3 oz) watercress, 3 tarragon sprigs, leaves stripped and torn, ¼ sliced cucumber, 2 tablespoons balsamic vinegar and 2 tablespoons extra virgin olive oil. Serve sprinkled with 2 tablespoons toasted pumpkin seeds and pepper. **Calories per serving 342**

chicken with spinach & ricotta

Calories per serving **441**
Serves **4**
Preparation time **10 minutes**
Cooking time **25 minutes**

4 **boneless, skinless chicken
breasts**, about 125 g (4 oz)
each
125 g (4 oz) **ricotta cheese**
125 g (4 oz) cooked **spinach**,
squeezed dry
¼ teaspoon **grated nutmeg**
8 slices of **Parma ham**
2 tablespoons **olive oil**, plus
extra for drizzling
salt and **pepper**

To serve
lemon wedges
rocket leaves

Make a long horizontal slit through the thickest part of each chicken breast without cutting right through.

Crumble the ricotta into a bowl. Chop the spinach and mix into the ricotta with the nutmeg. Season with salt and pepper.

Divide the stuffing between the slits in the chicken breasts and wrap each one in 2 pieces of Parma ham, winding it around the chicken to cover the meat totally.

Heat the oil in a shallow ovenproof pan, add the chicken breasts and cook for 4 minutes on each side, or until the ham starts to brown. Transfer to a preheated oven, 200°C (400°F), Gas Mark 6, and cook for 15 minutes until the chicken is cooked through. Serve with lemon wedges and rocket leaves drizzled with olive oil.

For chicken with mozzarella & sun-dried tomatoes, omit the ricotta, spinach and nutmeg, and stuff each chicken breast with a 40 g (1½ oz) slice of mozzarella cheese and a drained piece of sun-dried tomato. Season well with pepper and continue as above.
Calories per serving 471

butternut & coconut curry

Calories per serving **470**
Serves **4**
Preparation time **10 minutes**
Cooking time **30 minutes**

1 tablespoon **vegetable oil**
1 large **onion**, sliced
2 **green chillies**, deseeded
  and sliced
50 g (2 oz) **fresh root ginger**,
  peeled and grated
4 teaspoons **Thai curry paste**
2 **garlic cloves**, crushed
2 x 400 ml (14 fl oz) cans **low-**
  fat coconut milk
500 g (1 lb) **butternut**
  squash, peeled, deseeded
  and cut into bite-sized pieces
100 g (3½ oz) **red lentils**
200 g (7 oz) **baby spinach**
  leaves
bunch of **coriander**, chopped
400 g (13 oz) **cooked**
  basmati rice, to serve

Heat the oil in a saucepan, add the onion and fry for
3–4 minutes until softened, then add the chillies, ginger,
curry paste and garlic and cook, stirring, for a further
2 minutes.

Pour in the coconut milk and bring to the boil, then
add the squash. Reduce the heat and simmer for
12 minutes, then stir in the lentils and simmer for a
further 10 minutes until the squash is tender and the
lentils have softened.

Stir in the spinach leaves and coriander and cook for
2 minutes until wilted. Serve with the cooked rice.

For roasted butternut & lentil salad, toss 750 g
(1¾ lb) chopped butternut squash and 2 red onions,
cut into wedges, with 1 tablespoon olive oil, 1 crushed
garlic clove and 2 teaspoons thyme leaves. Roast in a
preheated oven, 200°C (400°F), Gas Mark 6, for
25– 30 minutes until tender. Meanwhile, whisk together
1 tablespoon balsamic vinegar, 1 tablespoon olive
oil and 1 teaspoon gluten-free wholegrain mustard
in a small bowl. Place 2 rinsed and drained 400 g
(13 oz) cans Puy lentils in a serving bowl, add 150 g
(5 oz) halved cherry tomatoes and 100 g (3½ oz) baby
spinach leaves, then toss with the dressing. Add the
roasted vegetables, toss again and serve sprinkled with
100 g (3½ oz) crumbled feta cheese. **Calories per
serving 376**

sausage & bean stew

Calories per serving **472**
Serves **4**
Preparation time **10 minutes**
Cooking time **20–25 minutes**

1 tablespoon **olive oil**
1 **onion**, chopped
2 **garlic cloves**, crushed
2 **carrots**, peeled and diced
4 good-quality **gluten-free sausages**
500 ml (17 fl oz) **gluten-free chicken stock**
400 g (13 oz) can **cherry tomatoes**
400 g (13 oz) can **butter beans**, rinsed and drained
200 g (7 oz) **Savoy cabbage**, thickly shredded
large bunch of **parsley**, chopped
salt and **pepper**
840 g (1¾ lb) **mashed potatoes**, to serve

Heat the oil in a large flameproof casserole, add the onion and fry for 4–5 minutes until softened, then add the garlic and carrots and cook for a further 2–3 minutes.

Add the sausages and cook for 6–8 minutes, turning occasionally, until just golden.

Pour in the stock, tomatoes, beans, cabbage and half the chopped parsley and simmer for 6–8 minutes until the sausages are cooked through and the cabbage is tender. Season to taste and sprinkle with the remaining parsley. Serve with the mashed potatoes.

For sausage & bean breakfast, chop the sausages into bite-sized pieces and cook in a frying pan with ½ tablespoon olive oil for 5–6 minutes until browned. Add the butter beans and cherry tomatoes, season and simmer for 10–12 minutes. Stir in 1 tablespoon chopped parsley, then make 4 dips in the mixture. Break 1 egg into each dip and cook for 6–8 minutes until the sausages and eggs are cooked through. (If you prefer your eggs cooked more, finish by placing the dish under the grill before serving.) **Calories per serving 309**

nasi goreng

Calories per serving **447**
Serves **4**
Preparation time **15 minutes**
Cooking time **10 minutes**

2 large **eggs**
3 tablespoons **sunflower oil**
1 tablespoon **tomato purée**
1 tablespoon **gluten-free
    ketjap manis** (sweet dark
    soy sauce)
625 g (1¼ lb) **cooked rice**
1 tablespoon **gluten-free light
    soy sauce**
5 cm (2 inch) piece of
    cucumber, quartered
    lengthways and sliced
8 **spring onions**, thinly sliced
    on the diagonal
salt and **pepper**

Spice paste
2 tablespoons **vegetable oil**
4 **garlic cloves**, roughly
    chopped
50 g (2 oz) **shallots**, roughly
    chopped
25 g (1 oz) **roasted salted
    peanuts**
6 **medium-hot red chillies**,
    deseeded and chopped
1 teaspoon **salt**

Make the spice paste. Place all of the ingredients
in a blender or food processor and whizz to a smooth
paste, or grind using a pestle and mortar.

Beat the eggs and season. Heat 1 tablespoon of
the sunflower oil in a small frying pan over a medium-
high heat, pour in a third of the beaten egg and cook
until set on top. Flip, cook for a few more seconds,
then turn out and roll up tightly. Repeat twice more
with the remaining egg. Slice the omelettes across
into thin strips.

Heat a wok over a high heat until smoking. Add
2 tablespoons of the oil and the spice paste and
stir-fry for 1–2 minutes. Add the tomato purée and
ketjap manis and cook for a few seconds, then tip
in the cooked rice and stir-fry over a high heat for
2 minutes until heated through.

Add the strips of omelette and stir-fry for a further
1 minute, then add the soy sauce, cucumber and most
of the spring onions and toss together well. Spoon
into 4 bowls, scatter over the remaining spring onions
and serve.

For quick spicy rice broth, tip 400 g (13 oz) cooked
rice into a saucepan with 200 ml (7 fl oz) coconut
milk, 600 ml (1 pint) hot gluten-free vegetable stock,
2 tablespoons tomato purée and 1 tablespoon mild
curry powder. Bring to the boil and cook over a high
heat for 4–5 minutes. Remove from the heat and stir
in 6 finely shredded spring onions and ¼ cucumber,
finely shredded. Season, ladle into 4 bowls and serve.
Calories per serving 245

turkey chilli

Calories per serving **499**
Serves **4**
Preparation time **15 minutes**
Cooking time 1¾ **hours**

1 tablespoon **olive oil**
2 **red onions**, chopped
1 **carrot**, peeled and diced
1 **celery stick**, diced
1 **red pepper**, cored,
   deseeded and chopped
1 **yellow pepper**, cored,
   deseeded and chopped
1 **red chilli**, deseeded and
   finely chopped
1 teaspoon **smoked paprika**
1 teaspoon **ground cumin**
bunch of **coriander**, roughly
   chopped
400 g (13 oz) **cooked
   turkey**, roughly chopped or
   shredded
400 g (13 oz) can **butter
   beans**, rinsed and drained
2 x 400 g (13 oz) can
   chopped tomatoes
juice of 1 **lime**
600 g (1¼ lb) **cooked
   basmati rice**, to serve

Heat the oil in a flameproof casserole, add the onions,
carrot, celery, peppers and chilli and cook for 5 minutes.
Add the paprika, cumin and chopped stalks of the
coriander, and cook for a further 5 minutes, stirring
occasionally, until the vegetables are softened. Add the
turkey, beans and tomatoes, mix well and cover with a lid.

Transfer to a preheated oven, 180°C (350°F), Gas
Mark 4, for 1½ hours, checking every 30 minutes and
adding a little water if it starts to look dry.

Remove from the oven, stir in the lime juice and
chopped coriander leaves. Serve with the cooked rice.

For turkey & rice noodle stir-fry, cook 300 g (10 oz)
rice noodles according to the packet instructions. Heat
1 teaspoon sunflower oil in a wok and fry 400 g (13 oz)
cooked turkey, sliced into strips, for 2 minutes. Add 325 g
(11 oz) trimmed green beans, 1 sliced red onion and
2 sliced garlic cloves and stir-fry for a further 4–5 minutes.
Stir in the juice of 1 lime, 1 teaspoon chilli powder,
1 diced red chilli and 1 tablespoon gluten-free fish
sauce. Add 1 tablespoon chopped mint, 2 tablespoons
chopped coriander and the drained rice noodles and
toss well before serving. **Calories per serving 441**

chicken kiev

Calories per serving **489**
Serves **4**
Preparation time **20 minutes,
    plus chilling**
Cooking time **40 minutes**

75g (3 oz) **butter**, softened
small handful of **parsley**, finely
    chopped
6 **garlic cloves**, crushed
grated rind of 2 **lemons**
4 **boneless, skinless chicken
    breasts**, about 150g (5 oz)
    each
4 slices of **gluten-free bread**
3 tablespoons **gluten-free
    plain flour**
3 **eggs**, beaten
salt and **pepper**
steamed **pak choi**, to serve

Mix together the butter, parsley, garlic and lemon rind
in a small bowl. Roll into 4 sausages, then cover and
place in the freezer for at least 30 minutes.

Slice the chicken breasts nearly in half horizontally.
Open like a book, then place between 2 sheets of
nonstick baking paper or clingfilm and flatten with a
rolling pin or mallet. Place 1 roll of garlic butter in the
centre of each breast, then wrap the breasts around the
butter, securing as tightly as possible with cocktail sticks.

Whizz the bread in a food processor to form breadcrumbs,
then tip into a shallow bowl. Place the flour on a plate
and season. Dip the rolled chicken breasts in the
seasoned flour, then the beaten egg and finally the
breadcrumbs until well coated. Roll again in the egg
and crumbs, if necessary.

Transfer the kievs to a baking sheet and place in a
preheated oven, 200° (400°F), Gas Mark 6, for
40 minutes until the chicken is golden and cooked
through. Serve with steamed pak choi.

nutty stuffed plaice parcels

Calories per serving **437**
Serves **4**
Preparation time **15 minutes**
Cooking time **20 minutes**

2 tablespoons **rapeseed oil**
75 g (3 oz) **chestnut
mushrooms**, chopped
75 g (3 oz) **roasted chopped
hazelnuts**
½ tablespoon chopped
parsley
4 **plaice fillets**, skinned
4 tablespoons **white wine**
25 g (1 oz) **butter**, cut into 4
pieces
400 g (13 oz) **new potatoes**,
halved
4 **Little Gem lettuces**,
quartered
1 tablespoon chopped **mint**
pepper

Heat 1 tablespoon of the oil in a frying pan, add the
mushrooms and cook for 5 minutes until softened.
Stir in the hazelnuts, then remove from the heat and
stir in the parsley.

Lay the plaice fillets on a clean surface and divide
the mushroom mixture between them, then roll up to
enclose the stuffing. Place each fillet on a piece of foil
large enough to enclose it, sprinkle with the white wine,
season with pepper, add 1 piece of the butter and seal
well. Bake in a preheated oven, 200°C (400°F), Gas
Mark 6, for 15 minutes, or until cooked through.

Meanwhile, cook the potatoes in a saucepan of
boiling water for 12–15 minutes until tender. Heat
the remaining oil in a frying pan, add the lettuce and
fry for 2–3 minutes on each side.

Drain the potatoes and season, then add the mint and
lightly crush with a fork. Top with the plaice parcels
and serve with the lettuce.

For plaice & mushrooms with hazelnut broccoli,
put 4 plaice fillets in an ovenproof dish and cover with
225 g (7½ oz) sliced mushrooms. Sprinkle with the
juice of 1 lemon and season. Dot with 25 g (1 oz) butter
and bake in a preheated oven, 180°C (350°F), Gas
Mark 4, for 16–17 minutes, basting frequently. Pour
over 150 ml (¼ pint) single cream and brown under a
preheated hot grill. Meanwhile, cook 350 g (11½ oz)
Tenderstem broccoli in a steamer for 3–4 minutes until
tender. Toss together with 2 tablespoons olive oil and
3 tablespoons chopped hazelnuts. Serve with the plaice.
Calories per serving 409

sea bass with spinach dhal

Calories per serving **438**
Serves **4**
Preparation time **5 minutes**
Cooking time **30 minutes**

1½ tablespoons **olive oil**
1 **onion**, finely diced
2 **garlic cloves**, finely chopped
1 **green chilli**, deseeded and
  finely chopped
1 teaspoon **mustard seeds**
1 teaspoon **cumin seeds**
2 teaspoons **garam masala**
200 g (7 oz) **red lentils**
400 g (13 oz) can **chopped
  tomatoes**
600 ml (1 pint) **gluten-free
  vegetable stock**
4 **sea bass fillets**, about
  150 g (5 oz) each
225 g (7½ oz) **spinach**
handful of **coriander leaves**,
  chopped
salt and **pepper**
1 tablespoon **toasted flaked
  almonds**, to garnish

Heat 1 tablespoon of the oil in a pan, add the onion
and fry for 5 minutes until soft. Stir in the garlic and
chilli and cook for a further 1 minute. Add the seeds
and garam masala and continue to cook for 2 minutes.

Stir in the lentils, tomatoes and stock and bring to the
boil. Reduce the heat and simmer for 20 minutes.

Meanwhile, heat the remaining oil in a separate large
frying pan and cook the sea bass for 3–4 minutes on
each side until cooked through.

Stir the spinach and chopped coriander through the
lentils until just starting to wilt, then season. Divide
the dhal between 4 plates and top each one with a sea
bass fillet. Serve sprinkled with toasted flaked almonds.

For grilled sea bass with garlicky spinach, cook
4 x 150 g (5 oz) sea bass fillets under a preheated hot
grill for 3–4 minutes on each side until cooked through.
Meanwhile, place 750 g (1¾ lb) spinach in a saucepan
and pour over a little boiling water, cover and cook for
1–2 minutes until the leaves start to wilt, then drain.
Heat 1 tablespoon olive oil in a large frying pan and
cook 3 tablespoons pine nuts and 2 chopped garlic
cloves for 2–3 minutes, then stir in the wilted spinach.
Divide between 4 plates and top with the sea bass
fillets. **Calories per serving 301**

creamy prawn curry

Calories per serving **482**
Serves **4**
Preparation time **5 minutes**
Cooking time **25–30 minutes**

1 tablespoon **sunflower oil**
1 **onion**, finely chopped
12 **curry leaves**
3 tablespoons **gluten-free
 curry paste**
200 ml (7 fl oz) **gluten-free
 fish stock**
600 ml (1 pint) **coconut milk**
300 g (10 oz) **green beans**,
 halved
400 g (13 oz) **raw peeled
 king prawns**
coriander leaves, to garnish

Heat the oil in a wok or large frying pan, add the onion and cook for 3–4 minutes until soft. Add the curry leaves and cook for a further 1 minute.

Stir in the curry paste and cook for 2 minutes, then pour in the stock and coconut milk and bring to the boil. Reduce the heat and simmer for 10–12 minutes.

Add the beans and cook for 5 minutes until just tender, then add the prawns and cook for a further 3 minutes until the prawns turn pink and are cooked through. Serve sprinkled with a few coriander leaves.

For spicy prawns, heat 1 tablespoon olive oil in a frying pan, add 3 peeled and chopped garlic cloves and 1 chopped red chilli and cook for 1 minute, then add 500 g (1 lb) raw peeled tiger prawns and cook for 3–4 minutes until the prawns turn pink and are cooked through. Serve on a bed of crisp lettuce leaves, sprinkled with the juice of 1 lime, pepper and a few coriander leaves. **Calories per serving 135**

bacon & leek tortilla

Calories per serving **483**
Serves **4**
Preparation time **10 minutes**
Cooking time **25–30 minutes**

4 tablespoons **olive oil**
2 **leeks**, trimmed, cleaned and
  thickly sliced
350 g (11½ oz) **new
  potatoes**, sliced
4 **back bacon rashers**,
  chopped
6 large **eggs**
75 g (3 oz) **mature Cheddar
  cheese**, grated
salt and **pepper**

Heat the oil in a large flameproof frying pan, add the leeks and potatoes and sauté for 8–10 minutes, stirring frequently, until golden and tender. Add the bacon and fry for a further 4–5 minutes until cooked through.

Meanwhile, beat the eggs in a large bowl and add the cheese. Season well.

Stir the potato mixture into the beaten eggs, then return to the pan and cook over a low heat for 8–10 minutes, making sure the bottom does not overcook.

Place the pan under a preheated hot grill and cook for a further 3–4 minutes until the tortilla is cooked through and golden. Serve cut into wedges.

For leek, butternut & bacon soup, heat 2 tablespoons olive oil in a saucepan, add 3 trimmed, cleaned and diced leeks and 400 g (13 oz) peeled, deseeded and diced butternut squash and cook for 3 minutes. Pour in 900 ml (1½ pints) hot gluten-free vegetable stock and bring to the boil, then reduce the heat and simmer for 4–5 minutes until the vegetables are soft. Meanwhile, cook 4 back bacon rashers under a preheated hot grill until crisp, then roughly chop. Stir 300 ml (½ pint) soya milk into the soup, then, using a hand-hand blender, blend the soup until smooth and season to taste. Ladle into 4 bowls and serve sprinkled with the bacon.
Calories per serving 249

turkey balls with minty quinoa

Calories per serving **474**
Serves **4**
Preparation time **10 minutes,
   plus cooling**
Cooking time **25 minutes**

2 tablespoons **olive oil**
1 **onion**, finely chopped
1 **garlic clove**, crushed
1 **courgette**, grated
400 g (13 oz) **minced turkey**
1 teaspoon **cumin seeds**
50 g (2 oz) **feta cheese**
20 g (¾ oz) **parsley**, chopped
250 g (8 oz) **quinoa**
200 g (7 oz) **frozen peas**
20 g (¾ oz) **mint**, chopped
grated rind and juice of 1
   lemon
100 g (3½ oz) **rocket leaves**

Heat ½ tablespoon of the oil in a frying pan, add the onion and garlic and fry for 4–5 minutes until softened, then leave to cool.

Mix together the cooked onion and garlic, courgette, turkey, cumin seeds, feta and half the parsley in a bowl. Shape into 12 balls and place on a baking sheet. Bake in a preheated oven, 200°C (400°F), Gas Mark 6, for 20 minutes until cooked through.

Meanwhile, cook the quinoa in a saucepan of boiling water according to the packet instructions. In a separate pan of boiling water, cook the peas until tender. Drain the quinoa and peas, then transfer to a bowl and stir in the mint, remaining parsley, lemon rind and juice and rocket leaves.

Serve the meatballs with the quinoa, drizzled with the remaining olive oil.

berry meringue mess

Calories per serving **475**
Serves **6**
Preparation time **10 minutes,**
  plus cooling
Cooking time **1** hour

3 **egg whites**
250 g (8 oz) **caster sugar**
1 teaspoon **white wine vinegar**
300 ml (½ pint) **double cream**
200 g (7 oz) **raspberries**, plus
  extra, left whole, to decorate
200 g (7 oz) **strawberries**,
  hulled and quartered,
  plus extra, left whole and
  unhulled, to decorate
2 tablespoons **icing sugar**
2 tablespoons **cream liqueur**

Line 2 large baking sheets with nonstick baking paper.

Whisk the egg whites in a large clean bowl until they form stiff peaks. Add the sugar a spoonful at a time and continue to whisk until thick and glossy. Fold in the vinegar with a large metal spoon.

Spoon or pipe 12 meringues on to the prepared baking sheets. Place in a preheated oven, 150°C (300°F), Gas Mark 2, for 1 hour, then switch off the oven and leave the meringues to cool completely. When cool, roughly crush the meringues.

Whip the cream in a large bowl until it forms soft peaks. Roughly crush together the raspberries and strawberries and stir into the cream. Fold in the crushed meringues, icing sugar and cream liqueur. Spoon into 6 tall glasses, decorate with extra berries and serve immediately.

For mango & passion fruit mess, make the meringues as above and roughly crush. Whip the cream with 2 tablespoons icing sugar in a large bowl until it forms soft peaks. Peel and stone 1 large mango and purée half the flesh in a food processor or blender. Chop the remaining mango flesh and stir all the mango into the cream mixture with the scooped flesh of 2 passion fruit. Fold in the crushed meringues and serve immediately.
Calories per serving 482

white chocolate risotto

Calories per serving **410**
Serves **6**
Preparation time **10 minutes**
Cooking time **25 minutes**

25 g (1 oz) **unsalted butter**
1 **vanilla pod**, split in half
lengthways
250 g (8 oz) **risotto rice**
4 tablespoons **caster sugar**
75 ml (3 fl oz) **white wine**
750 ml (1 ¼ pints) **milk**
75 g (3 oz) **gluten-free white
chocolate**, grated
6 **peaches**, halved and stoned

Melt the butter in a heavy-based saucepan. Scrape in the seeds from the vanilla pod and cook, stirring, for a few minutes. Stir in the rice and 2 tablespoons of the sugar and mix well. Pour in the wine, bring to the boil and cook, stirring constantly, until the liquid has been absorbed.

Add a little of the milk and gently simmer, stirring, until the milk has been absorbed. Continue to add the milk until the rice is soft but still holds its shape.

Remove the pan from the heat and stir in the grated chocolate, then cover and leave to stand.

Meanwhile, sprinkle the cut halves of the peaches with the remaining sugar and cook under a preheated grill until golden and bubbling.

Spoon the risotto into 6 serving bowls and top each with 2 grilled peach halves.

For quick peach & rice dessert, divide a drained 400 g (13 oz) can peaches in juice between 6 ramekins, then top with a 400 g (13 oz) can rice pudding. Sprinkle each one with ½ tablespoon demerara sugar and cook under a preheated grill until bubbling. Leave to cool before serving. **Calories per serving 157**

index

acknowledgements

Senior Commissioning Editor: Eleanor Maxfield
Project Editor: Clare Churly
Design and Art Direction: Geoff Fennell
Special Photography: William Shaw
Food Stylist: Joy Skipper
Prop Stylist: Liz Hippisley
Picture Library Manager: Jennifer Veall
Production Controller: Sarah Kramer

Special photography © Octopus Publishing Group
Limited/William Shaw. **Additional photography**
© Octopus Publishing Group Limited/Will Heap 67,
217; David Munns 105, 151, 155, 163; Sean Myers
41; Emma Neish 129, 143; Lis Parsons 11, 31, 75, 89,
99, 121, 147, 149, 167, 171, 187, 199, 205, 223, 229;
William Reavell 211; William Shaw 25, 29, 33, 35, 37,
39, 43, 45, 51, 53, 59, 63, 73, 81, 83, 87, 93, 113, 123,
125, 133, 135, 141, 159, 173, 175, 179, 181, 189,